I0866604

Building Spelling Skills

GRADE 3

What's in This Book?

Writing: Jo Ellen Moore
Content Editing: Leslie Sorg
Copy Editing: Cathy Harber
Art Direction: Cheryl Puckett
Cover Design: Cheryl Puckett
Illustration: Jim Palmer
Design/Production: Jia-Fang Eubanks
Yuki Meyer

EVAN-MOOR Educational Publishers

EMC 2707

Visit *teaching-standards.com* to view a correlation of this book.

Correlated to Current Standards

Congratulations on your purchase of some of the finest teaching materials in the world.

For information about other Evan-Moor products, call 1-800-777-4362, fax 1-800-777-4332, or visit our website, www.evan-moor.com.

10 Harris Court, Suite C-3, Monterey, CA 93940-5773. Printed in China.

010

CPSIA: Asia Pacific Offset Ltd, Kowloon, Hong Kong, China [3/2025]

Scope and Sequence

Teaching the Weekly Unit

Monday's Page

Monday

Allot ample class time each Monday for introducing the spelling list and having students complete the first page of the unit.

Introducing the Week's Words

Give each student the spelling list for the week. Here are ways to introduce the words:

- Call attention to important consistencies noted in "This Week's Focus," such as a phonetic or structural element. For example, say: *As we read this week's spelling list, notice that all the words have the same vowel sound.*
- Read each word aloud and have students repeat it.
- Provide a model sentence using the word. Have several students give their own sentences.
- If desired, add "bonus words" based on the needs of your class. These may be high-utility words or words that the class is encountering in curricular studies.

Writing the Words

After introducing the words, have students study and write the words on the first page of the unit, following these steps:

Step 1: Trace and Spell
Have students trace the word and spell it aloud.

Step 2: Copy and Spell
Tell students to copy the word onto the first blank line and spell it again, touching each letter as it is spoken.

Step 3: Cover and Spell
Have students fold the paper along the fold line to cover the spelling words so that only the last column shows. Then have students write the word from memory.

Step 4: Uncover and Check
Tell students to open the paper and check the spelling. Students should touch each letter of the word as they spell it aloud.

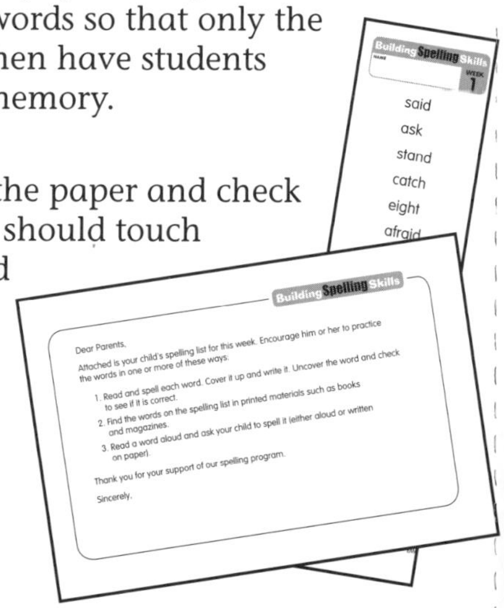

Home Connection

Send home a copy of the Parent Letter (page 145) and the Take-Home Spelling List for the week (pages 10–19).

Strengthening Students' Spelling Skills

Spelling Strategies
Page 6

How to Study Your List
Page 7

At the beginning of the year, reproduce pages 6 and 7 for each student or on an overhead transparency. Review the general steps and strategies, encouraging students to apply them throughout the year.

Tuesday Visual Memory Activities

Have students complete the activities on the second page of the unit. Depending on students' abilities, these activities may be completed as a group or independently.

Wednesday Word Meaning and Dictation

Have students complete the Word Meaning activity on the third page of the unit. Then use the dictation sentences on pages 8 and 9 to guide students through "My Spelling Dictation." Follow these steps:

1. Ask students to listen to the complete sentence as you read it.
2. Say the sentence in phrases, repeating each phrase one time clearly. Have students repeat the phrase.
3. Wait as students write the phrase.
4. When the whole sentence has been written, read it again, having students touch each word as you say it.

Thursday Word Study Activities

Have students complete the activities on the fourth page. Depending on students' abilities, these activities may be completed as a group or independently.

Friday Weekly Test

Friday provides students the chance to take the final test and to retake the dictation they did on Wednesday. A reproducible test form is provided on page 142. After the test, students can record their score on the "My Spelling Record" form (page 141).

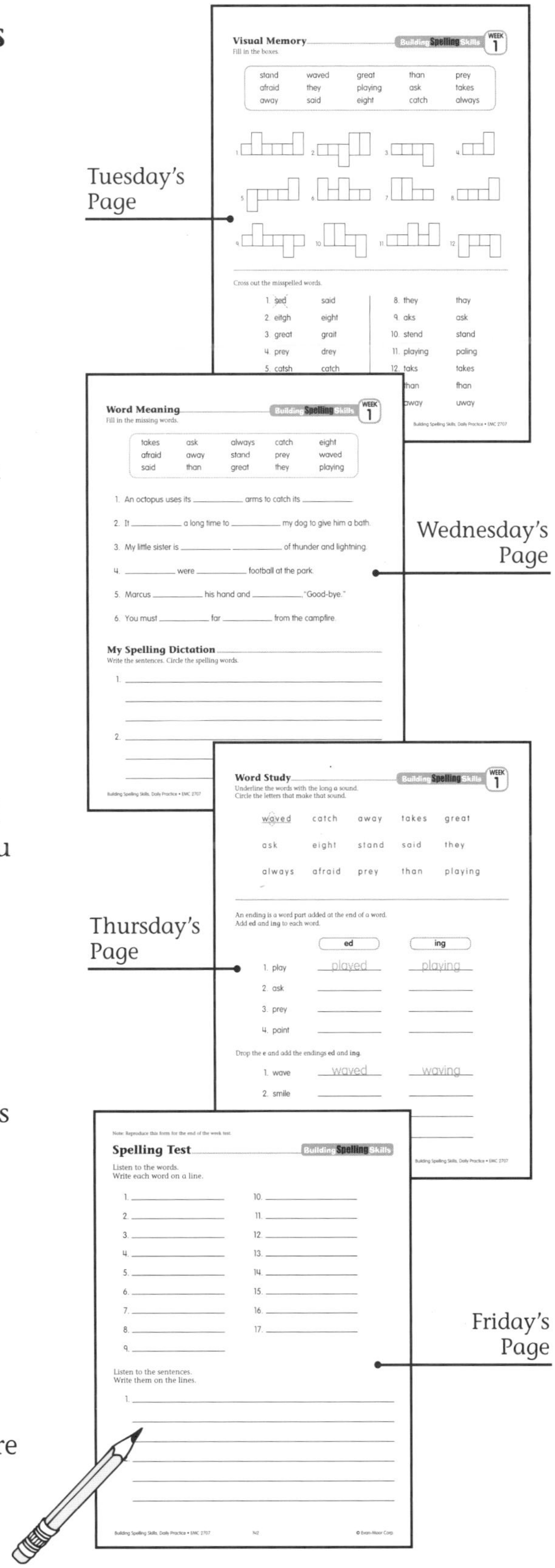

Spelling Strategies

Say a word correctly.

- Don't leave out or mispronounce sounds.
- Write the sounds in the correct order.

Think about what the word looks like.

- Think about how the spelling pattern looks.
- Write it, look at it, and decide if it looks correct.

Look for small words in spelling words.

- spin—**pin**, **in**
- cupcake—**cup**, **cake**

Look at syllables in spelling words.

- Spell the word one syllable at a time.
  remember—**re • mem • ber**

Use rhyming words to help spell a word.

- If you can spell **book**, you can spell **look**.

Use rules for adding endings.

- Drop silent **e** before adding a suffix.
- Double the final consonant before adding a suffix.
- Change the final **y** to **i** and add **es**.

How to Study Your List

1 Read and Spell

2 Copy and Spell

3 Cover and Spell

4 Uncover and Check

Sentences for Dictation

There are two dictation sentences for each spelling list. Space for sentence dictation is provided on Wednesday of each week and on Friday's test form (page 142).

- Ask students to listen to the complete sentence as you read it.
- Have students repeat the sentence.
- Read the sentence in phrases, repeating each phrase one time clearly.
- Have students repeat the phrase.
- Allow time for students to write the phrase.
- Read the sentence again, having students touch each word as you say it.

Week	Dictation Sentences
1	Were **they always playing** that **great** game? Jay is **afraid** of things with **eight** legs.
2	Has **she seen** the **sea very many** times? I **believe** I **left** my lunch **between** those seats.
3	Don't **swim while** the shark is close by. **Why** did you shine that **ligh**t in **my eye**?
4	Will your **pocket hold most** of the toy **rockets**? The king **often** sat on his gold **throne**.
5	**Touch** the **cute**, **young** kitten **under** its chin. Carlos invented a **new fuel** for **humans** to **use**.
6	The wind **blew** the **blue** kite **above** the trees. **Do** you **know** where you will **live** when you **move**?
7	Will the wind **carry** my **pretty balloon off** to **Mississippi**? Is the artist **willing** to draw a **different pattern**?
8	The note he **received** told who is **getting** the prize. Are you **coming** to the **swimming** party I'm **having**?
9	The **price** of **uniforms usually stayed** the same. Her **niece tried** to **float** an ice **cube**.
10	The **teacher** and her **children** went **everywhere together**. **Where** do you **think** we need to **search** for it?
11	**Everyone** came to school **without** their **homework today**. Was **everybody** scared by the **earthquake**?
12	That **tough** kid **called** the **small** boy an **awful** name. Bob **brought** his **strongest** rope **along** on our camping trip.
13	The **ladies cried** when the **story** was **finally** over. My **family** gave me **toys** and **shoes** as a **surprise**.

Week	Dictation Sentences
14	Is it **true** that the **school** has **good food**? Maggie **chewed** on **cookies** until she was **full**.
15	The **boy joined** his dad for a **voyage** across the sea. His **choice** was **oysters** and **chocolate** pudding for dinner.
16	**I'm** sure **we're** going where **they're** going. The clock **doesn't** work, so **they're** always late.
17	You **should follow** that **group** to the old **house**. My **cousin** ran **around town** until she **found** her dog.
18	Did **April's** pet rabbit have **those tiny white babies**? Pat **raised** the flag **over** her head.
19	I'm too **tired** to **read** the book **again**. **Does some of** the **money** need to be **given** to Mother?
20	**Clean** up the spilled **cereal** and put it in the **carton**. **Could** the **guards** save the **city** from **danger**?
21	Can I **learn** to be a **nurse** and **work** all around the **world**? Burt **stirred** the **fire** and **turned** the meat on the grill.
22	Farmer Brown takes **care** of her **large horse** every **morning**. **Aren't** you going to read the **warning** on the **chart**?
23	The **thoughtless** boy was cold **because** he **threw** away his jacket. It's **wonderful** to **watch water** flow over a cliff.
24	Take two **dollars** to the store and buy some **sugar**. **Doctor** Hunter said my leg will be **better** in **forty** days.
25	Her **nephew** was **unhappy** when he lost the **photograph**. **Happily**, his **cough** was better by **Friday**.
26	My **neighbor** thinks she saw a **ghost climb** on a tree **limb**. The postman **knew** the **wrong** name was **written** on the letter.
27	If you work too **quickly**, you will make **careless** mistakes. Everyone is **joyful** when Tina tells her **funniest** jokes.
28	I **heard Mother** call out a **friendly** greeting **early** this morning. **Measure** some milk and **break** an egg into the bowl.
29	**Our** mother **wrote** her letter on a **piece** of pretty paper. We must **wait** an **hour** for the bus that goes to **their** house.
30	It's **all right** to open the **beautiful presents** now. **People** went **straight** to the **hospital** after the train crash.

Building Spelling Skills

NAME

WEEK 1

said
ask
stand
catch
eight
afraid
away
always
playing
waved
takes
than
great
they
prey

bonus word

bonus word

cut

Building Spelling Skills

NAME

WEEK 2

next
left
help
please
believe
many
very
been
seen
she
between
three
easy
sea
leave

bonus word

bonus word

cut

Building Spelling Skills

NAME

WEEK 3

pitch
drink
swim
life
while
I
my
light
buy
eye
which
find
why
kind
try

bonus word

bonus word

Building Spelling Skills

NAME

WEEK 4

rocket
pocket
hold
told
often
grow
throne
so
sew
most
almost
both
coach
open
also

bonus word

bonus word

cut

Building Spelling Skills

NAME

WEEK 5

under
such
much
young
touch
use
your
you
unit
cute
few
new
fuel
human
music

bonus word

bonus word

cut

Building Spelling Skills

NAME

WEEK 6

save
give
have
live
move
above
alive
alike
to
two
too
know
do
blew
blue

bonus word

bonus word

Building Spelling Skills

NAME

WEEK 7

missed
willing
balloon
spelling
pretty
still
off
added
letter
different
pattern
middle
Mississippi
zipper
carry

bonus word

bonus word

cut

Building Spelling Skills

NAME

WEEK 8

swimming
swam
getting
coming
came
having
doing
ended
happened
happening
started
joked
received
smiled
smiling

bonus word

bonus word

cut

Building Spelling Skills

NAME

WEEK 9

way
these
niece
might
show
float
brain
mean
close
tried
cube
uniform
stayed
price
usually

bonus word

bonus word

Building Spelling Skills

NAME

WEEK 10

children
search
teacher
reached
think
together
with
where
everywhere
short
push
finish
sure
who
whole

bonus word

bonus word

cut

Building Spelling Skills

NAME

WEEK 11

into
today
without
something
become
upon
myself
everybody
everyone
maybe
outside
basketball
homework
skateboard
earthquake

bonus word

bonus word

© Evan-Moor Corporation • EMC 2707

cut

Building Spelling Skills

NAME

WEEK 12

awful
called
falling
mall
small
straw
drawing
strongest
longer
song
along
bought
brought
rough
tough

bonus word

bonus word

© Evan-Moor Corporation • EMC 2707

Building Spelling Skills

NAME

WEEK 13

lady
ladies
surprise
surprises
toys
shoes
shy
cry
cried
study
studied
story
only
finally
family

bonus word

bonus word

cut

Building Spelling Skills

NAME

WEEK 14

looked
good
brook
football
cookie
stood
full
put
food
school
truth
room
true
chew
due

bonus word

bonus word

cut

Building Spelling Skills

NAME

WEEK 15

pointing
oily
boy
voice
oyster
voyage
loyal
joined
coin
choice
poison
destroy
enjoy
choose
chocolate

bonus word

bonus word

Building Spelling Skills

NAME

WEEK 16

don't

didn't

I'll

I'm

it's

let's

you're

we're

doesn't

o'clock

won't

wouldn't

its

can't

that's

bonus word

bonus word

cut

Building Spelling Skills

NAME

WEEK 17

follow

below

own

grown

town

ground

around

found

about

house

group

would

should

country

cousin

bonus word

bonus word

cut

Building Spelling Skills

NAME

WEEK 18

April

babies

over

hello

even

we

silent

tiny

menu

future

dear

raise

white

used

those

bonus word

bonus word

Building Spelling Skills

NAME

WEEK 19

disagree
again
given
other
money
problem
does
of
some
laid
change
tired
read
nice
lower

bonus word

bonus word

cut

Building Spelling Skills

NAME

WEEK 20

city
cereal
face
could
guess
huge
age
danger
goose
gone
coast
clean
guard
giant
carton

bonus word

bonus word

cut

Building Spelling Skills

NAME

WEEK 21

word
work
world
were
first
girl
turned
learn
bird
fire
here
nurse
jury
stirred
wear

bonus word

bonus word

Building Spelling Skills

NAME

WEEK 22

aren't

partner

hard

chart

farm

start

large

more

before

horse

north

morning

care

stare

warning

____
bonus word

____
bonus word

cut

Building Spelling Skills

NAME

WEEK 23

threw

through

thoughtless

caught

fault

taught

because

one

once

water

watch

wanted

wonder

wonderful

walk

____
bonus word

____
bonus word

cut

Building Spelling Skills

NAME

WEEK 24

color

odor

farmer

calendar

dollar

party

liar

after

number

better

doctor

weather

every

forty

sugar

____
bonus word

____
bonus word

Building Spelling Skills

NAME

WEEK 25

phone
photograph
orphan
alphabet
graph
nephew
enough
father
half
Friday
cough
unhappy
happier
happily
happiness

bonus word

bonus word

cut

Building Spelling Skills

NAME

WEEK 26

ghost
neighbor
high
knew
knot
unknown
rewrap
wrong
written
wrapper
unwrap
climb
limb
gnaw
gnat

bonus word

bonus word

cut

Building Spelling Skills

NAME

WEEK 27

useful
quietly
slowly
careful
careless
quickly
useless
worthless
fearful
fearless
joyful
smarter
fastest
funniest
happiest

bonus word

bonus word

Building Spelling Skills

NAME

WEEK 28

brother
mother
another
field
friend
heard
early
friendly
head
near
year
shield
eat
measure
break

bonus word

bonus word

cut

Building Spelling Skills

NAME

WEEK 29

they're
there
their
soup
night
knight
right
write
weight
wait
piece
peace
hour
our
wrote

bonus word

bonus word

cut

Building Spelling Skills

NAME

WEEK 30

air
against
all right
until
presents
beautiful
favorite
clothes
people
vacation
remember
already
hospital
minute
straight

bonus word

bonus word

Building Spelling Skills WEEK 1

Spelling List

This Week's Focus:

- Spell short and long **a** words
- Spell words with the endings **-ed** and **-ing**
- Add the endings **-ed** and **-ing** after dropping the silent **e**
- Recognize the short **e** sound in **said**

STEP 1 Read and Spell	STEP 2 Copy and Spell	STEP 3 Cover and Spell
1. said	______	______
2. ask	______	______
3. stand	______	______
4. catch	______	______
5. eight	______	______
6. afraid	______	______
7. away	______	______
8. always	______	______
9. playing	______	______
10. waved	______	______
11. takes	______	______
12. than	______	______
13. great	______	______
14. they	______	______
15. prey	______	______
16. ______ bonus word	______	______
17. ______ bonus word	______	______

fold

Visual Memory

Fill in the boxes.

stand	waved	great	than	prey
afraid	they	playing	ask	takes
away	said	eight	catch	always

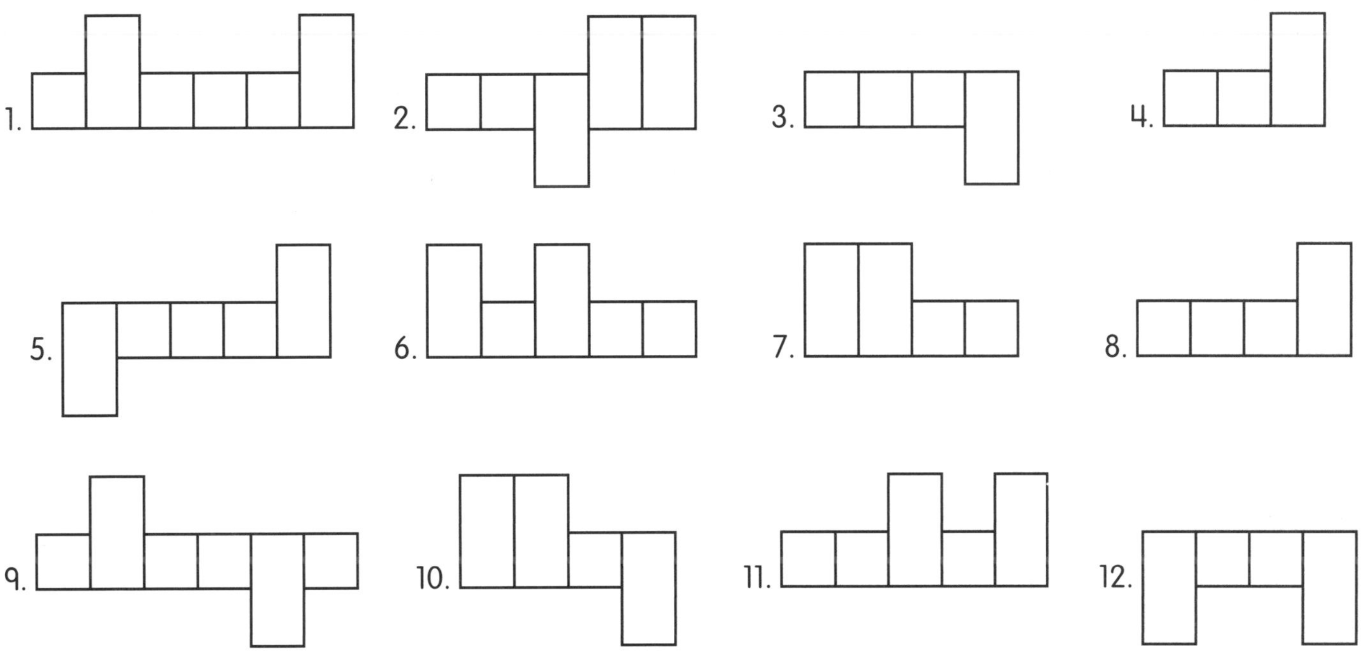

Cross out the misspelled words.

1. sed	said	8. they	thay
2. eitgh	eight	9. aks	ask
3. great	grait	10. stend	stand
4. prey	drey	11. playing	paling
5. catsh	catch	12. taks	takes
6. afraid	ufraid	13. than	fhan
7. wavd	waved	14. away	uway

Word Meaning

Fill in the missing words.

takes	ask	always	catch	eight
afraid	away	stand	prey	waved
said	than	great	they	playing

1. An octopus uses its ____________ arms to catch its ____________.
2. It ____________ a long time to ____________ my dog to give him a bath.
3. My little sister is ____________ ____________ of thunder and lightning.
4. ____________ were ____________ football at the park.
5. Marcus ____________ his hand and ____________, "Good-bye."
6. You must ____________ far ____________ from the campfire.

My Spelling Dictation

Write the sentences. Circle the spelling words.

1. ____

____

____

2. ____

____

____

Word Study

Underline the words with the long **a** sound.
Circle the letters that make that sound.

waved	catch	away	takes	great
ask	eight	stand	said	they
always	afraid	prey	than	playing

An ending is a word part added at the end of a word.
Add **ed** and **ing** to each word.

	ed	ing
1. play	played	playing
2. ask		
3. prey		
4. paint		

Drop the **e** and add the endings **ed** and **ing**.

1. wave	waved	waving
2. smile		
3. skate		
4. bake		

Building Spelling Skills WEEK 2

Spelling List

This Week's Focus:

- Spell short **e** words
- Spell words with the long **e** sound spelled **ea**, **ie**, **ee**, **e**, and **y**
- Recognize the short **i** sound in **been**

STEP 1 Read and Spell	STEP 2 Copy and Spell	STEP 3 Cover and Spell
1. next	______	______
2. left	______	______
3. help	______	______
4. please	______	______
5. believe	______	______
6. many	______	______
7. very	______	______
8. been	______	______
9. seen	______	______
10. she	______	______
11. between	______	______
12. three	______	______
13. easy	______	______
14. sea	______	______
15. leave	______	______
16. ______ bonus word	______	______
17. ______ bonus word	______	______

fold

Visual Memory

Fill in the boxes.

very	believe	next	easy	leave
been	please	help	between	she
seen	many	left	three	sea

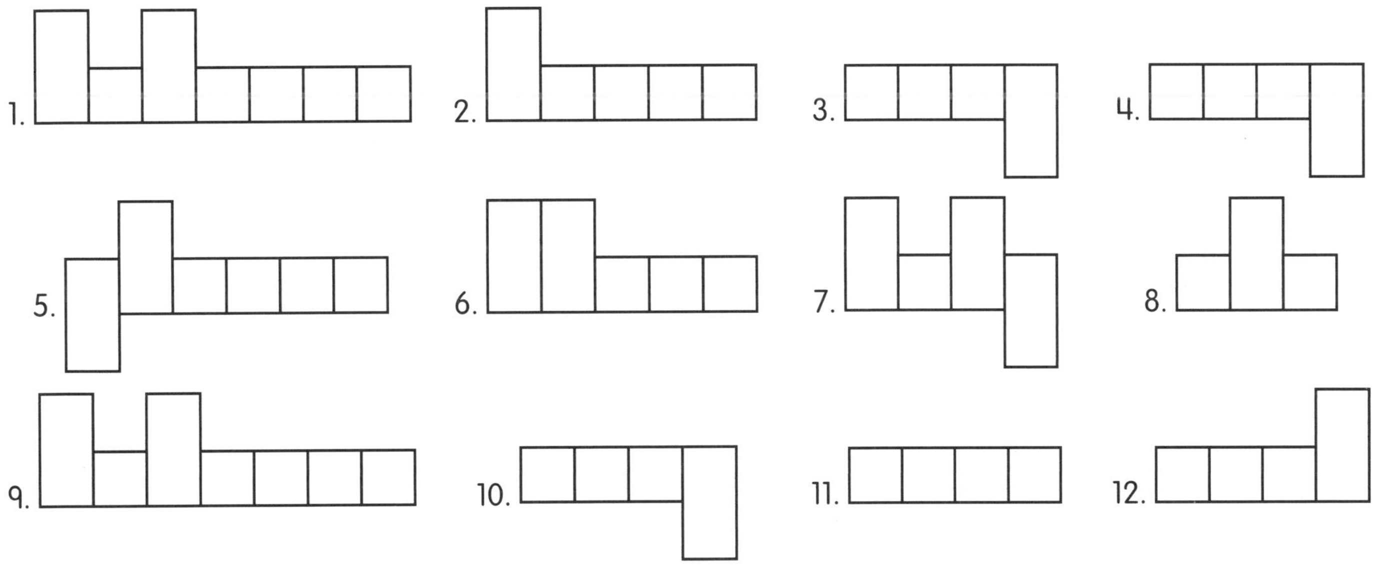

Circle the misspelled words. Write them correctly on the lines.

1. Plez help me fix my bike. ________________
2. We have to leaf now. ________________
3. It isn't eezy to ride a horse. ________________
4. Have you ben to the park? ________________
5. Park the car betwene the trees. ________________
6. Did you belive his story? ________________
7. I saw miny cows at his farm. ________________
8. Jane had tree pet cats. ________________

Word Meaning

Answer the questions.

next	left	help	please	believe
many	very	been	seen	she
between	three	easy	sea	leave

1. What comes after **two**? ______
2. What is another word for **ocean**? ______
3. What is the opposite of... ?

   difficult ______ stay ______

   right ______ harm ______

   few ______
4. Which word means "in the middle of two things"? ______
5. What word do you use if you want to show good manners? ______
6. Which word means you think something is true? ______

My Spelling Dictation

Write the sentences. Circle the spelling words.

1. ______

2. ______

Word Study

Underline the words with the long **e** sound.
Circle the letters that make that sound.

three	left	she
please	believe	many
very	been	seen
help	between	leave
easy	sea	next

Write the spelling words that rhyme with these words.

1. merry ____________
2. any ____________
3. sneeze ____________
4. free ____________
5. yelp ____________
6. pea ____________
7. queen ____________
8. relieve ____________
9. bee ____________
10. lean ____________

next	left	help	please	believe
many	very	been	seen	she
leave	three	easy	sea	between

Building Spelling Skills WEEK 3

Spelling List

This Week's Focus:

- Spell short and long **i** words
- Spell words in the **-ind**, **-ile**, **-ight**, and **-ink** word families

STEP 1 Read and Spell	STEP 2 Copy and Spell	STEP 3 Cover and Spell
1. pitch		
2. drink		
3. swim		
4. life		
5. while		
6. I		
7. my		
8. light		
9. buy		
10. eye		
11. which		
12. find		
13. why		
14. kind		
15. try		
16. ______ bonus word		
17. ______ bonus word		

fold

Visual Memory

Fill in the boxes.

life	pitch	my	eye	why
drink	while	light	which	kind
try	I	buy	find	swim

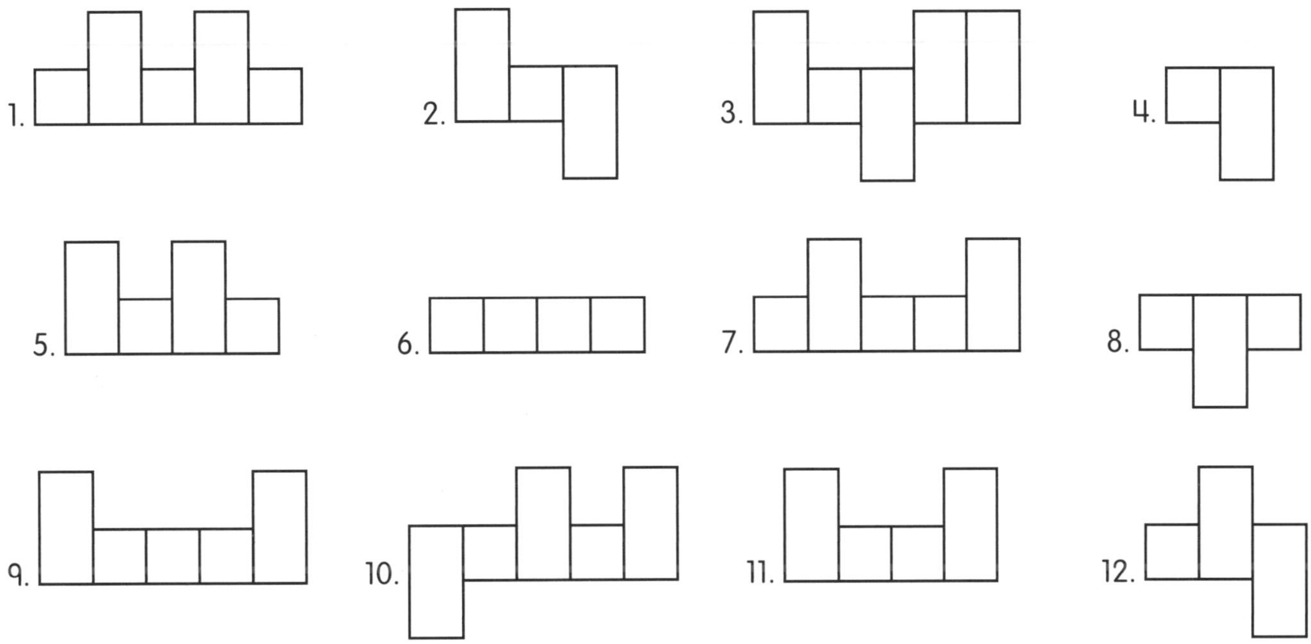

Circle the misspelled words.
Write them correctly on the lines.

1. Mom needs to bie a lite for the lamp. __________ __________
2. Witch kind of drenk do you like best? __________ __________
3. Trie to catch the ball when I picth it. __________ __________
4. I get water in my aye when I swem. __________ __________
5. Eye like to by that kind of pen. __________ __________

Word Meaning

Fill in the missing words.

1. ____________ (I, try) have something in my ____________ (why, eye).

2. ____________ (Why, Try) did you ____________ (buy, which) that kind of soft ____________ (drink, pitch)?

3. ____________ (Which, Witch) kind of ____________ (while, light) do you need?

4. Can you catch ____________ (while, light) I ____________ (why, pitch) the baseball?

5. The words ____________ (my, find) and ____________ (try, while) rhyme.

6. I have tried to be a ____________ (find, kind) person all of my ____________ (while, life).

My Spelling Dictation

Write the sentences. Circle the spelling words.

1. ____

____

____

2. ____

____

____

Word Study

Underline the words with the long **i** sound.
Circle the letters that make that sound.

life	drink	try
pitch	while	I
my	light	buy
eye	which	find
why	kind	swim

Add letters to make new words.
Then read all the words in each word family.

ind	ile	ight	ink
____f ind	____ile	____ight	____ink
____ind	____ile	____ight	____ink
____ind	____ile	____ight	____ink
____ind	____ile	____ight	____ink

Building Spelling Skills WEEK 4

Spelling List

This Week's Focus:

- Spell words with the long **o** sound
- Distinguish between one- and two-syllable words

STEP 1 Read and Spell	STEP 2 Copy and Spell	STEP 3 Cover and Spell
1. rocket	________	________
2. pocket	________	________
3. hold	________	________
4. told	________	________
5. often	________	________
6. grow	________	________
7. throne	________	________
8. so	________	________
9. sew	________	________
10. most	________	________
11. almost	________	________
12. both	________	________
13. coach	________	________
14. open	________	________
15. also	________	________
16. ________ bonus word	________	________
17. ________ bonus word	________	________

fold

Visual Memory

Fill in the boxes.

rocket	hold	often	grow	so
pocket	told	also	sew	most
throne	almost	both	coach	open

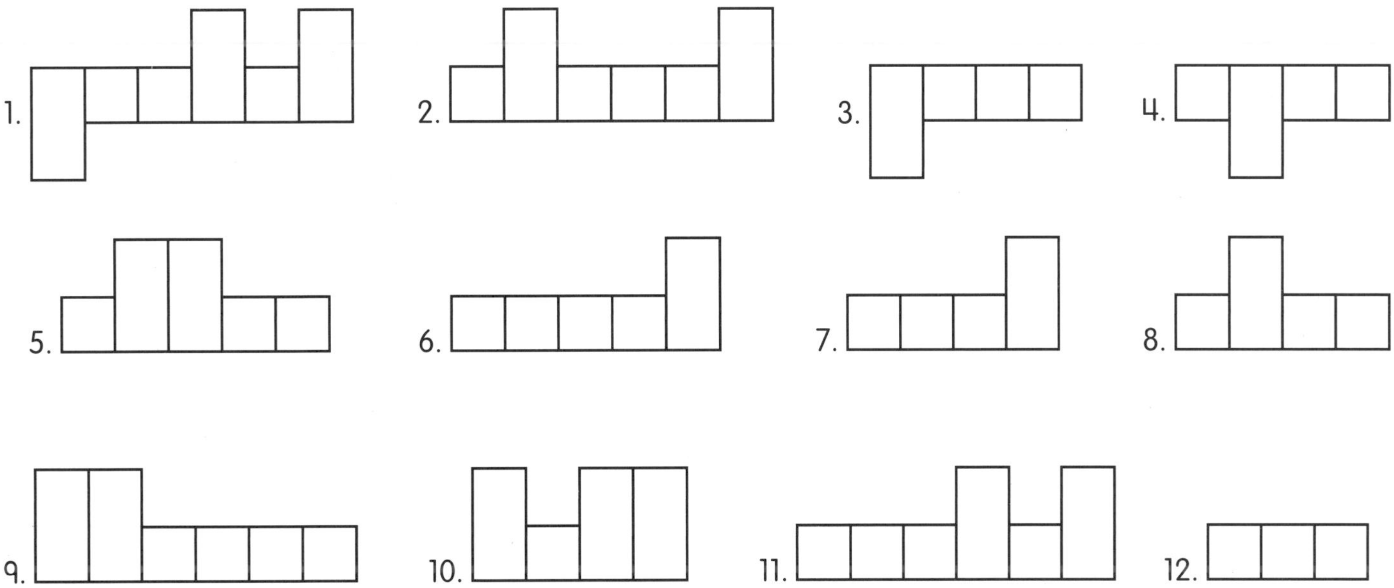

Cross out the misspelled words.

1.	roket	rocket	7.	coach	koach
2.	whold	hold	8.	allso	also
3.	often	offen	9.	opun	open
4.	throne	thone	10.	grow	groe
5.	amolst	almost	11.	told	tole
6.	both	bofh	12.	sowe	sew

Word Meaning

Answer the questions.

rocket	hold	often	grow	so
pocket	most	also	sew	told
throne	almost	both	coach	open

1. What could a king or queen sit on? ____________
2. In what part of a jacket can you carry things? ____________
3. Which two spelling words rhyme with **cold**?

   ____________ ____________

4. Which two spelling words sound the same but have different spellings?

   ____________ ____________

5. What is the opposite of **shut**? ____________
6. What transportation would an astronaut use? ____________

My Spelling Dictation

Write the sentences. Circle the spelling words.

1. ____________________________________

2. ____________________________________

Word Study

Underline the words with the long **o** sound.
Circle the letters that make that sound.

grow	hold	throne
rocket	so	pocket
told	also	sew
most	often	almost
both	coach	open

Say each word.

rocket	hold	often	both	almost
grow	so	pocket	coach	throne
told	also	sew	open	most

Write the words with one syllable.

1. ______________________
2. ______________________
3. ______________________
4. ______________________
5. ______________________
6. ______________________
7. ______________________
8. ______________________
9. ______________________

Write the words with two syllables.

1. ______________________
2. ______________________
3. ______________________
4. ______________________
5. ______________________
6. ______________________

Building Spelling Skills WEEK 5

Spelling List

This Week's Focus:

- Spell words with the short and long **u** sounds
- Spell words with an initial /**y**/ sound

STEP 1 Read and Spell	STEP 2 Copy and Spell	STEP 3 Cover and Spell
1. under	______	______
2. such	______	______
3. much	______	______
4. young	______	______
5. touch	______	______
6. use	______	______
7. your	______	______
8. you	______	______
9. unit	______	______
10. cute	______	______
11. few	______	______
12. new	______	______
13. fuel	______	______
14. human	______	______
15. music	______	______
16. ______ bonus word	______	______
17. ______ bonus word	______	______

fold

Visual Memory

Unscramble the letters to make spelling words.

under	such	much	young	touch
use	your	you	unit	fuel
few	new	cute	human	music

1. chum ______________
2. outch ______________
3. sue ______________
4. uoy ______________
5. intu ______________
6. wef ______________
7. lufe ______________
8. redun ______________
9. chus ______________
10. hunam ______________
11. sicmu ______________
12. gnuoy ______________

Circle the misspelled words. Write them correctly on the lines.

1. Jim's dog ran undar the bed. ______________
2. Do you like her noo coat? ______________
3. What is yer name? ______________
4. That's a kute baby. ______________
5. Don't tuch the hot stove! ______________
6. Ann's sister is a yung lady. ______________
7. A fuo boys came to the party. ______________
8. Do you like rap moosic? ______________

Word Meaning

Draw a picture to show what each sentence means.

Kate found her kitten hiding under the bed.	Dad pumped fuel into the tank of his new car.
The young boy played music.	A few pennies were in the cute piggy bank.

My Spelling Dictation

Write the sentences. Circle the spelling words.

1. ______________________________

____

____

2. ______________________________

____

____

Word Study

Underline the words with the long **u** sound.
Circle the letters that make that sound.

use	such	few
young	music	under
your	you	unit
cute	much	new
fuel	human	touch

Write the spelling words that rhyme with these words.

1. crutch	____________	6. flute	____________
2. sung	____________	7. few	____________
3. thunder	____________	8. jewel	____________
4. shoes	____________	9. Dutch	____________
5. too	____________	10. store	____________

Fill in the blanks with rhyming word pairs from above.

1. Zeke hid ____________ the bed when he heard ____________.
2. They bought a ____________ pairs of ____________ shoes.
3. A ____________ little girl played music on her ____________.

Building Spelling Skills WEEK 6

Spelling List

This Week's Focus:

- Spell words that end with a silent **e**
- Spell homophones
- Compare past and present tense verbs

STEP 1 Read and Spell | **STEP 2 Copy and Spell** | **STEP 3 Cover and Spell**

fold

1. save
2. give
3. have
4. live
5. move
6. above
7. alive
8. alike
9. to
10. two
11. too
12. know
13. do
14. blew
15. blue
16. ______________ bonus word
17. ______________ bonus word

Visual Memory

Fill in the missing letters.

save	give	have	live	move
above	alike	alive	to	two
too	know	do	blew	blue

_____oo _____ike _____ew _____ow

_____ue _____wo _____o _____o

_____ove _____ove _____ave _____ave

_____ive _____ive _____ive

Circle the misspelled words.
Write them correctly on the lines.

1. There were tow plants in the pot. ____________
2. The girls looked ulike. ____________
3. His new bike is blew. ____________
4. Do you no what fish like to eat? ____________
5. May I hav a ride to school? ____________
6. Will you geve me some milk? ____________
7. Nat went too the zoo. ____________
8. Moov your bike out of the street. ____________

Word Meaning

Homophones are words that sound alike but have different spellings and meanings.

Choose the correct homophone for each sentence.

1. That little boy is _______________ years old.
   (to, two, too)
2. I want an ice-cream cone, _______________.
   (to, two, too)
3. Bring the plates _______________ the table.
   (to, two, too)
4. A strong wind _______________ the leaves off the trees.
   (blew, blue)
5. Did you see how _______________ the sky was today?
   (blew, blue)
6. When will you _______________ if you can go on the trip?
   (know, no)
7. There is _______________ more peanut butter in the jar.
   (know, no)

My Spelling Dictation

Write the sentences. Circle the spelling words.

1. ______________________________

   ____

   ____

2. ______________________________

   ____

   ____

Word Study

A present tense verb tells about what is happening **NOW**.
A past tense verb tells about what happened before.
Use the spelling list to find the present tense for each past tense verb.
Write the present tense words on the lines.

past tense	present tense	past tense	present tense
1. gave	______________	5. did	______________
2. moved	______________	6. had	______________
3. lived	______________	7. saved	______________
4. knew	______________		

Fill in the correct verb form.

1. New people just ______________ (move) in next door.
2. Do you ______________ (know) how to make toast?
3. The man ______________ (blow) up balloons and made animals out of them.
4. Have you ______________ (save) the money you need for a new bike?

Draw lines to match these words to their opposites.

alive	different
alike	below
above	dead

Building Spelling Skills WEEK 7

Spelling List

This Week's Focus:
- Spell words with double consonants
- Divide words into syllables

STEP 1 Read and Spell	STEP 2 Copy and Spell	STEP 3 Cover and Spell
1. missed		
2. willing		
3. balloon		
4. spelling		
5. pretty		
6. still		
7. off		
8. added		
9. letter		
10. different		
11. pattern		
12. middle		
13. Mississippi		
14. zipper		
15. carry		
16. ______ bonus word		
17. ______ bonus word		

fold

Visual Memory

Find the words hiding in this puzzle.

m	b	a	l	l	o	o	n	o	f	f	x	l
i	i	l	l	z	i	p	m	i	d	d	l	e
s	o	s	w	i	l	l	i	n	g	i	z	t
s	c	a	s	s	y	z	g	o	o	f	a	t
e	t	s	t	i	l	l	i	u	v	f	d	e
d	g	i	p	a	s	l	i	p	p	e	d	r
c	o	l	r	o	w	s	n	o	p	r	e	p
a	z	l	e	t	t	r	i	n	e	e	d	r
r	p	a	t	t	e	r	n	p	l	n	r	e
r	o	p	t	d	i	f	f	u	p	t	z	t
y	f	e	y	o	s	p	e	l	l	i	n	g

- added
- balloon
- carry
- different
- letter
- middle
- missed
- Mississippi
- off
- pattern
- pretty
- spelling
- still
- willing
- zipper

Circle the correct spelling.

1. misst	missed	mised	missd
2. baloon	balon	ballon	balloon
3. pretty	pertty	preddy	prety
4. ledder	eter	leter	letter
5. differunt	different	diferent	diffrent
6. patturn	patern	pattern	pattren
7. carry	cerry	karry	kerry
8. ziper	zippir	zipper	zippre

Word Meaning

Fill in the missing words.

added	balloon	carry	different	pattern
middle	missed	off	Mississippi	letter
pretty	spelling	still	willing	zipper

1. Did you study for the ________________ test?
2. We sailed on the ________________ River.
3. I bought a shiny red ________________ for my little sister.
4. The ________________ on her jacket broke.
5. Will you help me ________________ this box into the house?
6. Who wrote you that ________________?
7. I went to a ________________ school last year.
8. Mother cut out the ________________ for a new dress she is making.

My Spelling Dictation

Write the sentences. Circle the spelling words.

1. ____

____

____

2. ____

____

____

Word Study

Divide these words into syllables.
Remember the rules:

- If a word has double consonants in the middle, divide between them.
- If a word has an ending, divide between the base word and the ending.

1. balloon bal loon
2. spelling spell ing
3. pretty ______
4. letter ______
5. added ______
6. pattern ______
7. zipper ______
8. willing ______
9. middle ______
10. carry ______
11. missing ______
12. Mississippi ______

Fill in the missing double consonants to make spelling words.

1. spe____ing
2. o____
3. sti____
4. mi____le
5. pa____ern
6. mi____ed
7. di____erent
8. Mi____i____i____i

Building Spelling Skills WEEK 8

Spelling List

This Week's Focus:

- Spell verbs that end with **-ing** or **-ed**
- Spell irregular past tense verbs

STEP 1 Read and Spell	STEP 2 Copy and Spell	STEP 3 Cover and Spell
1. swimming		
2. swam		
3. getting		
4. coming		
5. came		
6. having		
7. doing		
8. ended		
9. happened		
10. happening		
11. started		
12. joked		
13. received		
14. smiled		
15. smiling		
16. ______ bonus word		
17. ______ bonus word		

fold

Visual Memory

Circle the missing letters. Fill in the blanks.

1. swi__mm__ing m (mm)
2. ca______e m mm
3. ge______ing t tt
4. star______ed t tt
5. en______ed d dd
6. ha______ened p pp
7. smi______ed l ll
8. sti______ l ll
9. swa______ m mm
10. co______ing m mm
11. jo______ed k kk
12. recei______ed v vv

Write the correct spelling of these words.

1. swiming ____________
2. geting ____________
3. comeng ____________
4. haveng ____________
5. dooing ____________
6. happend ____________
7. happining ____________
8. joket ____________
9. smild ____________
10. kame ____________

Fill in the missing word. Use the correct ending.

1. Raul ____________ (start) piano lessons last week.
2. Have you ____________ (receive) your birthday present yet?
3. Why is she ____________ (smile)?

Word Meaning

Fill in the correct form of the missing words.

1. We ____________ in the river yesterday.
   (swam, swimming)

2. They are going ____________ today.
   (swam, swimming)

3. What is ____________ on that television program?
   (happened, happening)

4. That is the same thing that ____________ on the last show.
   (happened, happening)

5. Who is ____________ to the band concert?
   (came, coming)

6. Many people ____________ to hear us play last year.
   (came, coming)

7. Karen ____________ when she opened the front door.
   (smiling, smiled)

8. Why was she ____________?
   (smiling, smiled)

My Spelling Dictation

Write the sentences. Circle the spelling words.

1. ____

____

____

2. ____

____

____

Word Study

Write the past tense of these words.
Use the spelling list.

1. joke ____________
2. swim ____________
3. happen ____________
4. come ____________
5. end ____________
6. smile ____________
7. receive ____________
8. start ____________

Add the ending **ing** to each base word.
What did you do to spell the word correctly?

	no change	double final consonant	drop **e**
1. swimming		✔	
2. get________			
3. receive________			
4. come________			
5. have________			
6. do________			
7. smile________			
8. end________			
9. happen________			
10. start________			
11. joke________			

Building Spelling Skills WEEK 9

Spelling List

This Week's Focus:

- Spell words with long vowel sounds
- Add **-ed** to verbs

STEP 1 **Read and Spell** | STEP 2 **Copy and Spell** | STEP 3 **Cover and Spell**

fold

1. way ____________ ____________
2. these ____________ ____________
3. niece ____________ ____________
4. might ____________ ____________
5. show ____________ ____________
6. float ____________ ____________
7. brain ____________ ____________
8. mean ____________ ____________
9. close ____________ ____________
10. tried ____________ ____________
11. cube ____________ ____________
12. uniform ____________ ____________
13. stayed ____________ ____________
14. price ____________ ____________
15. usually ____________ ____________
16. ____________ (bonus word) ____________ ____________
17. ____________ (bonus word) ____________ ____________

Visual Memory

Unscramble the words.
Match them to the correct spelling.

1. yaw	close	8. beuc	price
2. thees	niece	9. ripce	float
3. neice	way	10. mitgh	cube
4. hows	these	11. foalt	uniform
5. anme	tried	12. niarb	brain
6. locse	mean	13. formuni	stayed
7. deirt	show	14. edstay	might

Circle the misspelled words.
Write them correctly on the lines.

1. My new band youniform is silver. ____________
2. Cloze the door when you go out. ____________
3. The boys mite go fishing next Saturday. ____________
4. Put an ice kube in that glass. ____________
5. Grandpa staid in bed until 8 o'clock. ____________
6. The fox tryed to catch a rabbit. ____________
7. Can you shoo me how to play this game? ____________
8. Did you ever drink a root beer flote? ____________

Word Meaning

Complete the crossword puzzle.

Across

1. not kind
4. the cost
5. special clothing
8. to shut
9. this one and this one

Down

2. a girl relative
3. what you think with
6. the opposite of **sink**
7. a six-sided square
10. to remain

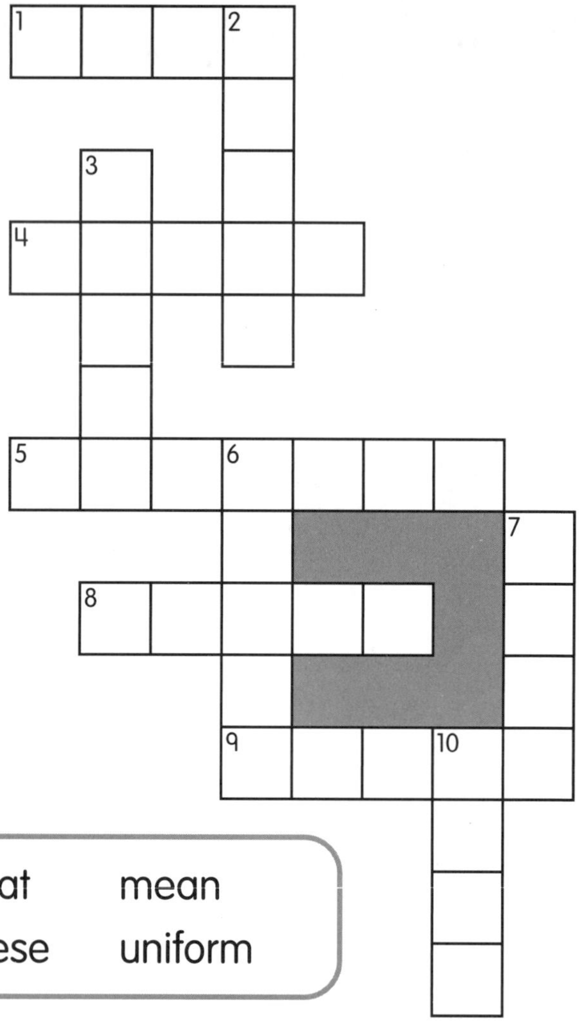

brain	close	cube	float	mean
niece	price	stay	these	uniform

My Spelling Dictation

Write the sentences. Circle the spelling words.

1. ____________________

2. ____________________

Word Study

Circle the letters that make the long vowel sound.
Write the long vowel sound you hear on the line.

1. way <u>a</u>	6. brain ____	11. uniform ____
2. these ____	7. mean ____	12. stayed ____
3. niece ____	8. close ____	13. price ____
4. show ____	9. tried ____	
5. float ____	10. cube ____	

Add **ed** to the words. Write the words in the correct column.

	no change	change **y** to **i**
1. stay	stayed	
2. try		
3. float		
4. show		
5. cry		
6. hurry		
7. plant		
8. worry		
9. play		
10. scurry		

Building Spelling Skills WEEK 10

Spelling List

This Week's Focus:

- Spell words with consonant digraphs **ch**, **sh**, **th**, and **wh**
- Identify the number of syllables in a word
- Recognize the /**sh**/ sound in **sure**

STEP 1 Read and Spell	STEP 2 Copy and Spell	STEP 3 Cover and Spell
1. children		
2. search		
3. teacher		
4. reached		
5. think		
6. together		
7. with		
8. where		
9. everywhere		
10. short		
11. push		
12. finish		
13. sure		
14. who		
15. whole		
16. ____ bonus word		
17. ____ bonus word		

fold

Visual Memory

Circle all the words that are spelled correctly.

reacht	finush	search
teatcher	whol	where
children	with	chilren
whith	shure	who
think	push	serch
everywere	sure	teacher
whole	poosh	thinck

Circle the misspelled words.
Write them correctly on the lines.

1. Hoo ate that hole cake?

    ________________ ________________

2. Can the childrun poosh the wagon?

    ________________ ________________

3. We can go when you finnish the shurt story.

    ________________ ________________

4. Where do you tink we should serch for it?

    ________________ ________________

5. Will you and your teecher go there togepher?

    ________________ ________________

Word Meaning

Answer the questions.

children	search	teacher	reached	think
together	with	where	short	push
everywhere	finish	sure	who	whole

1. Which ones are names for people?

   ______________ ______________

2. Which word means "all places"? ______________

3. What do you do when you use your brain? ______________

4. Which word means "to complete something"? ______________

5. Which word means "to look for something that is lost"? ______________

6. What is the opposite of...?

   part ______________ long ______________ apart ______________

My Spelling Dictation

Write the sentences. Circle the spelling words.

1. ______________________________

   ____

   ____

2. ______________________________

   ____

   ____

Word Study

Fill in the missing letters to make spelling words.
Write **ch**, **th**, **wh**, or **sh**.

1. ch ildren
2. sear____
3. ____ink
4. ____ole
5. ____ere
6. fini____
7. toge____er
8. pu____
9. tea____er
10. wi____
11. ____ort
12. ____o

Read the words.
Circle the number of syllables you hear.

1. together 1 2 3 4
2. who 1 2 3 4
3. search 1 2 3 4
4. teacher 1 2 3 4
5. reached 1 2 3 4
6. think 1 2 3 4
7. with 1 2 3 4
8. everywhere 1 2 3 4
9. sure 1 2 3 4
10. children 1 2 3 4
11. whole 1 2 3 4
12. finish 1 2 3 4
13. push 1 2 3 4
14. where 1 2 3 4
15. short 1 2 3 4

Building Spelling Skills WEEK 11

Spelling List

This Week's Focus:
- Spell compound words
- Divide compound words into syllables

STEP 1 Read and Spell	STEP 2 Copy and Spell	STEP 3 Cover and Spell
1. into		
2. today		
3. without		
4. something		
5. become		
6. upon		
7. myself		
8. everybody		
9. everyone		
10. maybe		
11. outside		
12. basketball		
13. homework		
14. skateboard		
15. earthquake		
16. ______ bonus word		
17. ______ bonus word		

fold

Visual Memory

Building Spelling Skills **WEEK 11**

Find the words hiding in this puzzle.

e v e r y b o d y e s s
v a n h o m e w o r k o
e r r t o d a y m a a m
r w i t h o u t y b t e
y o u i h e r o s e e t
o u t n o q u d e c b h
n e w t t u u y l o o i
e u p o n t o a f m a n
m a y b e m y s k e r g
o u t o u t s i d e d o
b a s k e t b a l l i n

become
basketball
earthquake
everybody
everyone
homework
into
maybe
myself
outside
skateboard
something
today
upon
without

Circle the 10 misspelled words.
Write them correctly on the lines.

Yesterday I finished my homewerk by misef. Then I went owtside and rode my skatbord to the park. Everbody was playing baskutball.

Evrywon was having fun when sumthing happened. The ground started to shake. It was an erthquak! When it stopped, we ran home wifout the basketball. Maybe it is still at the park.

Word Meaning

Fill in the missing words.

become	basketball	upon	into	everyone
homework	skateboard	maybe	myself	outside
something	earthquake	today	without	everybody

1. Maurice received a ______________ for his birthday.
2. An ______________ made cracks in the walls of our house.
3. Our teacher said, "There is no ______________ ______________!"
4. ______________ strange ran ______________ the barn.
5. Once ______________ a time, there was a dragon that couldn't fly.
6. Do you want to ______________ a professional soccer player someday?
7. Can you wash the car ______________ any help?
8. ______________ is gone, so I am all by ______________.

My Spelling Dictation

Write the sentences. Circle the spelling words.

1. ____

____

____

2. ____

____

____

Word Study

Building Spelling Skills WEEK 11

Use the words in the word box to make compound words.

with	up	to	thing	quake
board	ball	day	every	body
come	side	my	may	home

1. basketball________
2. be________
3. earth________
4. every________
5. ________one
6. ________work
7. in________
8. ________self
9. ________be
10. out________
11. skate________
12. some________
13. to________
14. ________on
15. ________out

Divide these words into syllables.

1. in|to
2. today
3. without
4. become
5. something
6. maybe
7. outside
8. homework
9. earthquake

Did you discover a new rule here about dividing words into syllables? Yes No

What is it? ________________

Building Spelling Skills WEEK 12

Spelling List

This Week's Focus:

- Spell words with the vowel sound in **small**, **straw**, **song**, and **bought**
- Spell words with the short **u** sound spelled **ough**
- Add the endings **-er** and **-est**

STEP 1 Read and Spell	STEP 2 Copy and Spell	STEP 3 Cover and Spell
1. awful		
2. called		
3. falling		
4. mall		
5. small		
6. straw		
7. drawing		
8. strongest		
9. longer		
10. song		
11. along		
12. bought		
13. brought		
14. rough		
15. tough		
16. ______ bonus word		
17. ______ bonus word		

fold

Visual Memory

Unscramble the words. Write them on the lines.

falling	awful	called	mall	straw
small	drawing	strongest	longer	tough
song	along	bought	brought	rough

1. awflu __________
2. decall __________
3. llam __________
4. gons __________
5. malls __________
6. olang __________
7. rouhg __________
8. lnoger __________
9. traws __________
10. darwing __________
11. srongtest __________
12. flaling __________

Circle the misspelled words. Write them correctly on the lines.

1. Adam made an ahful mistake.

   ____

2. Put the smal starw in the cold drink.

   __________ __________

3. He made a drawn of the stronust man in the world.

   __________ __________

4. Anna bawght it at the moll.

   __________ __________

5. Will you sing a longar sogn next time?

   __________ __________

Word Meaning

Answer the questions.

falling	awful	called	mall	straw
small	drawing	strongest	longer	tough
song	along	bought	brought	rough

1. Which word means "terrible"? ____________
2. What could be used to make a bed for a farm animal? ____________
3. What do you call a place with many shops all together? ____________
4. Which word is a kind of picture? ____________
5. What is the opposite of...?

   sold ____________ shorter ____________

   large ____________ weakest ____________

6. What does **straw** mean in this sentence? Circle your answer.

   I used a plastic straw to drink my milk.

   a. dried hay b. thin, hollow tube c. material for making popcorn

My Spelling Dictation

Write the sentences. Circle the spelling words.

1. ____________

2. ____________

Word Study

Underline the words with the sound of **a** in **all**.
Circle the letters that make the sound.

awful	called	tough
mall	song	along
rough	bought	straw
strongest	falling	brought
small	drawing	longer

Add **er** or **est** to make a comparison.

	er	est
1. strong	________	________
2. long	________	________
3. small	________	________
4. rough	________	________
5. tough	________	________

6. That wrestler is the ________ (strong) man I've ever seen.
7. Is a rabbit ________ (small) than a cat?
8. Mrs. Martin has the ________ (rough) bath towels I've ever felt.
9. Billy thinks he is the ________ (tough) kid on our block.
10. The yellow bus is ________ (long) than our truck.

Building Spelling Skills WEEK 13

Spelling List

This Week's Focus:

- Spell words with the long **e** and long **i** sounds spelled **y**
- Spell the plural forms of words by adding **s**, **es**, or **ies**
- Spell the past tense of words by changing **y** to **i** and adding **ed**

STEP 1 Read and Spell	STEP 2 Copy and Spell	STEP 3 Cover and Spell
1. lady		
2. ladies		
3. surprise		
4. surprises		
5. toys		
6. shoes		
7. shy		
8. cry		
9. cried		
10. study		
11. studied		
12. story		
13. only		
14. finally		
15. family		
16. ______ bonus word		
17. ______ bonus word		

fold

Visual Memory

Fill in the missing syllable to make spelling words.

1. la<u>dy</u>______
2. ________ily
3. on________
4. ________prises
5. ________dies
6. stud________
7. fi________ly
8. ________y
9. ________ied
10. sur________

Circle the misspelled words.
Write them correctly on the lines.

1. The children gave Mother a big suprise. ________
2. Put on your shoos before you go outside. ________
3. The baby cryed for his bottle. ________
4. Do you have a big famuly? ________
5. Two ladys sang a song. ________
6. Did you enjoy the storie? ________
7. The game was finelly over. ________
8. Have you studyed for the math test? ________

Word Meaning

Fill in the missing words.

1. What __________ was in that large box?
   (surprise, surprises)

2. Both __________ bought new hats.
   (lady, ladies)

3. Did he __________ clean his bedroom?
   (finally, family)

4. She wants to __________ the violin.
   (study, studied)

5. My grandfather is full of funny __________ that make me laugh.
   (surprise, surprises)

6. I __________ for a long time when my best friend moved away.
   (cry, cried)

My Spelling Dictation

Write the sentences. Circle the spelling words.

1. ______________________________

____

____

2. ______________________________

____

____

Word Study

Write the words in the correct boxes.

cry	only	story	my	study	fly
lady	why	family	funny	shy	try

y says **i**	**y** says **e**
cry	

Write the plural forms. Mark how you changed each word.

		add **s**	drop **e**, add **es**	change **y** to **i** and add **es**
1. lady	ladies			✔
2. toy				
3. story				
4. shoe				
5. family				
6. rocket				
7. niece				

Building Spelling Skills WEEK 14

Spelling List

This Week's Focus:

- Spell words with the vowel sounds in **push** and **do**

STEP 1 Read and Spell	STEP 2 Copy and Spell	STEP 3 Cover and Spell
1. looked		
2. good		
3. brook		
4. football		
5. cookie		
6. stood		
7. full		
8. put		
9. food		
10. school		
11. truth		
12. room		
13. true		
14. chew		
15. due		
16. ____ bonus word		
17. ____ bonus word		

fold

Visual Memory

Find the words hiding in the puzzle.

f	g	t	r	u	t	h	c	h	f
l	o	o	k	e	d	r	o	c	u
f	o	o	d	o	o	k	o	o	l
t	d	p	t	c	h	e	w	o	l
r	u	u	u	b	r	o	o	k	m
u	e	s	p	t	a	t	h	i	h
e	s	c	h	o	o	l	x	e	e
n	o	s	t	o	o	d	l	m	w

brook	looked
chew	put
cookie	room
due	school
food	stood
football	true
full	truth
good	

Circle the misspelled words.
Write them correctly on the lines.

1. luked
2. good
3. brook
4. futbal
5. cookee
6. fud
7. full
8. poot
9. stood
10. schol
11. truth
12. doo
13. chu
14. true
15. ruum

______________ ______________ ______________

______________ ______________ ______________

______________ ______________ ______________

Word Meaning

Complete the crossword puzzle.

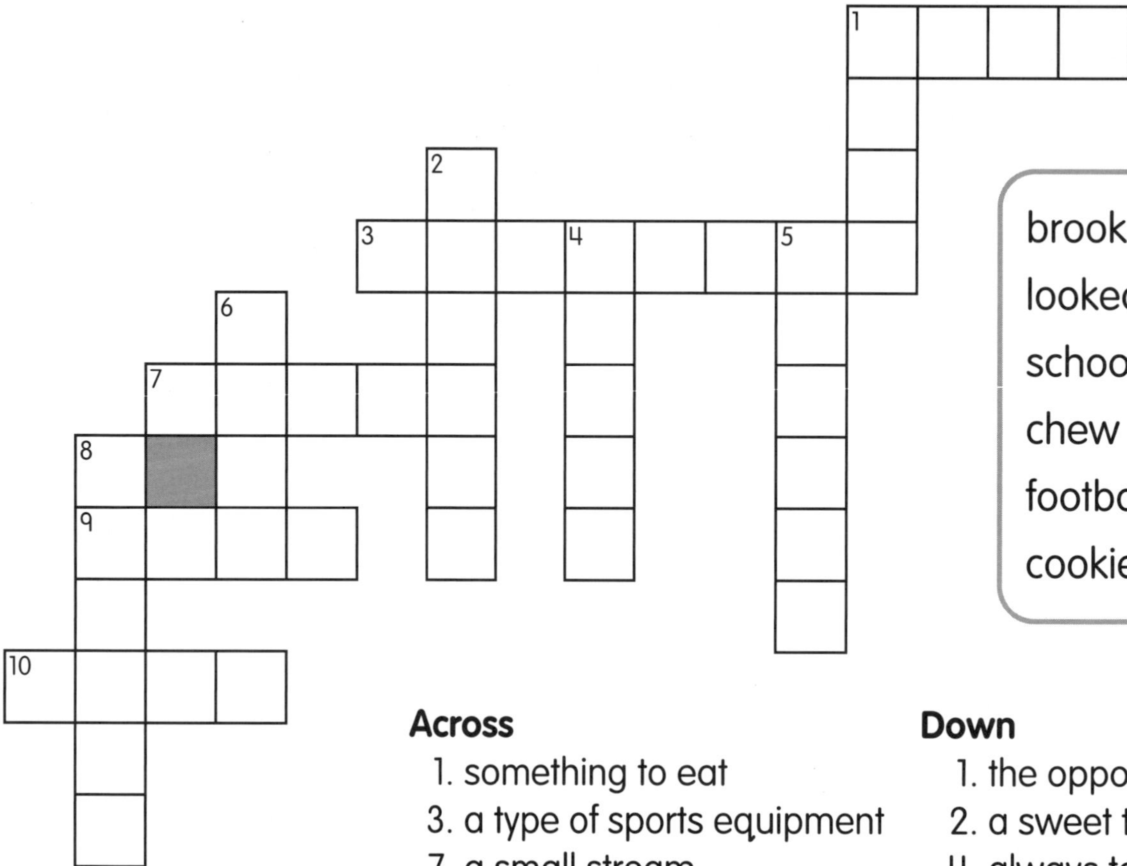

brook	food
looked	full
school	true
chew	truth
football	good
cookie	

Across

1. something to eat
3. a type of sports equipment
7. a small stream
9. to crush with your teeth
10. the opposite of **bad**

Down

1. the opposite of **empty**
2. a sweet treat
4. always tell the ____
5. used your eyes to see
6. not a lie
8. where you go to learn

My Spelling Dictation

Write the sentences. Circle the spelling words.

1. ____________________

2. ____________________

Word Study

Write the words in the correct boxes.

looked	good	truth	put	stood
food	brook	room	true	full
football	school	cookie	chew	due

sound of **u** in **push**	sound of **o** in **do**
looked	

Use the spelling list to find words that are the opposite.

1. empty ____________
2. awful ____________
3. sat ____________
4. remove ____________
5. lie ____________
6. false ____________

Building Spelling Skills WEEK 15

Spelling List

This Week's Focus:

- Spell words with **oy** and **oi**
- Spell words with the initial digraph **ch**
- Add the endings **-s**, **-es**, **-ed**, and **-ing**

STEP 1 Read and Spell	STEP 2 Copy and Spell	STEP 3 Cover and Spell
1. pointing	______	______
2. oily	______	______
3. boy	______	______
4. voice	______	______
5. oyster	______	______
6. voyage	______	______
7. loyal	______	______
8. joined	______	______
9. coin	______	______
10. choice	______	______
11. poison	______	______
12. destroy	______	______
13. enjoy	______	______
14. choose	______	______
15. chocolate	______	______
16. ______ bonus word	______	______
17. ______ bonus word	______	______

fold

Visual Memory

Unscramble the words. Match them to the correct spelling.

1. yoil	voice	8. ocin	coin
2. cevoi	oily	9. ingpoint	joined
3. soyter	boy	10. cocholate	choice
4. joyen	voyage	11. edjoin	chocolate
5. yob	oyster	12. oichce	pointing
6. agevoy	loyal	13. sonpoi	destroy
7. loyla	enjoy	14. troydes	poison

Circle the misspelled words. Write them correctly on the lines.

1. My choyse is chocklate.

   ________________ ________________

2. Did you injoy your voyege?

   ________________ ________________

3. He will distroy the weeds without using poisen.

   ________________ ________________

4. The little doy is pointing at an oister.

   ________________ ________________

5. Which coyn did he chose?

   ________________ ________________

Word Meaning

Fill in the missing words.

1. We ate ________________ on our sea ________________.
   (coins, oysters) (poison, voyage)

2. ________________ cake is always Paul's ________________.
   (Oyster, Chocolate) (choose, choice)

3. Did that ________________ ________________ his toy truck?
   (joined, boy) (destroy, loyal)

4. Why are you ________________ at that gold ________________?
   (pointing, oily) (joined, coin)

5. Don't use a loud ________________ while the baby is taking a nap.
   (choice, voice)

6. Lock the box of insect ________________ in a cupboard.
   (chocolate, poison)

My Spelling Dictation

Write the sentences. Circle the spelling words.

1. ____

____

____

2. ____

____

____

Word Study

Fill in the missing sounds. Write **oi** or **oy**.

1. b_____	4. _____ster	7. p_____son	10. c_____n
2. _____ly	5. v_____ce	8. p_____nting	11. enj_____
3. ch_____ce	6. l_____al	9. destr_____	12. j_____ned

Add endings to change the verbs.

	s or es	ed	ing
1. point	points	_____	_____
2. join	_____	_____	_____
3. smile	_____	_____	_____
4. finish	_____	_____	_____

Add the correct endings to the verbs.

1. Norman was _____ (smile) at the funny television show.
2. The short hand on a clock always _____ (point) to the hour.
3. Betty always _____ (finish) her work before she plays.
4. Carlos is _____ (join) the Boy Scouts.

Building Spelling Skills WEEK 16

Spelling List

This Week's Focus:
- Spell contractions
- Recognize homophones **it's** and **its**

Step 1 Read and Spell	Step 2 Copy and Spell	Step 3 Cover and Spell
1. don't		
2. didn't		
3. I'll		
4. I'm		
5. it's		
6. let's		
7. you're		
8. we're		
9. doesn't		
10. o'clock		
11. won't		
12. wouldn't		
13. its		
14. can't		
15. that's		
16. ______ bonus word		
17. ______ bonus word		

fold

Visual Memory

A contraction is a word formed from two words by leaving out some letters. An apostrophe is used to replace the letters.

Write the apostrophe in the correct place in these contractions.

1. don't
2. didnt
3. Ill
4. thats
5. its
6. cant
7. lets
8. youre
9. were
10. doesnt
11. oclock
12. wont
13. Im
14. wouldnt

Circle the misspelled words.
Write them correctly on the lines.

1. They din't like the scary movie. ____________
2. Did you know were moving when school is out? ____________
3. Why duzn't the clock work? ____________
4. Your going to Disneyland next week! ____________
5. Tat's Cindy's pet hamster. ____________
6. Its too hot to play outside today. ____________
7. Let's ask why they kan't come over. ____________
8. A'll bring my football to the game. ____________

Word Meaning

Write the contractions to complete the crossword puzzle. Don't forget to include the apostrophe.

Down

1. cannot
2. I will
3. does not
5. do not
6. of the clock
7. it is
8. we are

Across

4. would not
8. will not
9. that is
10. you are
11. let us

My Spelling Dictation

Write the sentences. Circle the spelling words.

1. ______________________________

____

____

2. ______________________________

____

____

Word Study

Answer the questions.

1. What is the long form of these words?

   won't ______________ don't ______________

2. Which spelling means "belonging to it"? its it's

3. Which spelling means "I will"? Ill I'll

What letter or letters are removed to make the contraction?

	contractions	missing letters
1. do not	don't	o
2. we are		
3. they are		
4. it is		
5. would not		
6. cannot		
7. I am		
8. that is		
9. does not		
10. did not		
11. I will		
12. let us		

Building Spelling Skills WEEK 17

Spelling List

This Week's Focus:

- Spell words with the vowel digraphs **ow** and **ou**

STEP 1 Read and Spell | **STEP 2 Copy and Spell** | **STEP 3 Cover and Spell**

(fold)

1. follow
2. below
3. own
4. grown
5. town
6. ground
7. around
8. found
9. about
10. house
11. group
12. would
13. should
14. country
15. cousin
16. ______ bonus word
17. ______ bonus word

Visual Memory

Fill in the missing letters. Write **ou** or **ow**.

1. t______n	6. c______sin	11. ar______nd
2. h______se	7. ab______t	12. gr______n
3. gr______p	8. ______n	13. c______ntry
4. f______nd	9. bel______	14. sh______ld
5. foll______	10. w______ld	15. gr______nd

Circle the 9 misspelled words in the paragraph.
Write them correctly on the lines.

My kussin went on a hike with a grup of children from toun. They fallowed a path bello a small hill. They walked arownd a grove of trees and saw a herd of cows resting on the groun. Then it was time for everyone to go to my cuzin's howse for lunch.

__________ __________ __________

__________ __________ __________

__________ __________ __________

Word Meaning

Fill in the missing words.

1. The prairie dog ________ (below, town) is under the ________ (country, ground).

2. My ________ (cousin, group) lives in a ________ (country, around) across the ocean.

3. A large ________ (own, group) of visitors stayed at our ________ (house, cousin).

4. The farmer's corn crop ________ (around, should) be ________ (own, grown) by now.

5. Kelly looked all ________ (around, ground) trying to find her lost shoe.

6. Do you have your ________ (town, own) computer at home?

My Spelling Dictation

Write the sentences. Circle the spelling words.

1. ____

____

____

2. ____

____

____

Word Study

Listen for the vowel sounds.
Write the words in the correct boxes.

grown	group	ground	about	below
town	follow	would	own	should
found	country	around	cousin	house

sound of **o** in **go**	sound of **ow** in **cow**	sound of **oo** in **too**	sound of **u** in **up**	sound of **u** in **put**

Use words from the spelling list to make rhyming words.

1. shout ______________
2. mouse ______________
3. dozen ______________
4. soup ______________
5. could ______________ ______________
6. show ______________ ______________
7. ground ______________ ______________
8. bone ______________ ______________

Building Spelling Skills WEEK 18

Spelling List

This Week's Focus:

- Review words with long vowel sounds
- Identify long vowels in open syllables

STEP 1 Read and Spell	STEP 2 Copy and Spell	STEP 3 Cover and Spell
1. April		
2. babies		
3. over		
4. hello		
5. even		
6. we		
7. silent		
8. tiny		
9. menu		
10. future		
11. dear		
12. raise		
13. white		
14. used		
15. those		
16. ______ bonus word		
17. ______ bonus word		

fold

Visual Memory

Match the parts to make words.
Write the words correctly on the lines.

1. A	ver	1. April
2. e	pril	2.
3. ba	ny	3.
4. si	u	4.
5. o	bies	5.
6. ti	ven	6.
7. men	lent	7.
8. fu	ture	8.

Circle the misspelled words.
Write the words correctly on the lines.

1. My grandmother says all babys are deer.

2. Mr. Martin is going to raize tiney roses in his garden.

3. It was sylent in the cave until someone yelled, "Heloo!"

4. Last Aprul we painted our fence whyte.

5. The teacher yousd thoze books in her class.

Word Meaning

Answer the questions.

April	babies	over	hello	even
we	silent	tiny	menu	future
dear	raise	white	used	those

1. What do you use to choose a meal at a restaurant? ____________

2. Which word means...?

   time that hasn't happened yet ____________

   above something ____________

   not new ____________

   a greeting ____________

   no sound ____________

3. How do you change the word **baby** to make it mean "more than one baby"? ____________

4. What month comes after March? ____________

My Spelling Dictation

Write the sentences. Circle the spelling words.

1. ______________________________

____

____

2. ______________________________

____

____

Word Study

Read the words. Listen for a long vowel sound.
Write the words in the correct boxes.

April	raised	used	over	babies
tiny	menu	those	silent	hello
we	white	future	even	

long **a**	long **o**	long **e**	long **i**	long **u**

An open syllable has a vowel at the end. The vowel is usually long.
Divide these words into syllables.
Circle the open syllable or syllables in each word.

1. April (A) pril
2. babies ________ ________
3. over ________ ________
4. hello ________ ________
5. even ________ ________
6. lady ________ ________
7. silent ________ ________
8. tiny ________ ________
9. menu ________ ________
10. future ________ ________

Bonus: vacation ________ ________ ________

Building Spelling Skills WEEK 19

Spelling List

This Week's Focus:

- Spell words with the short **u** sound
- Spell words with the schwa sound
- Review words with long vowel sounds

STEP 1 Read and Spell	STEP 2 Copy and Spell	STEP 3 Cover and Spell
1. disagree	________	________
2. again	________	________
3. given	________	________
4. other	________	________
5. money	________	________
6. problem	________	________
7. does	________	________
8. of	________	________
9. some	________	________
10. laid	________	________
11. change	________	________
12. tired	________	________
13. read	________	________
14. nice	________	________
15. lower	________	________
16. ________ bonus word	________	________
17. ________ bonus word	________	________

fold

Visual Memory

Find the words hiding in this puzzle.

a	g	a	i	n	c	h	a	n	g	e	p
l	a	i	d	p	r	o	n	i	o	x	r
o	o	s	v	o	u	t	t	c	c	f	o
w	m	o	n	e	y	h	r	e	a	d	b
e	e	m	g	q	n	e	b	y	n	o	l
r	h	e	e	t	i	r	e	d	t	e	e
a	g	d	i	s	a	g	r	e	e	s	m

again	nice
change	of
disagree	other
does	problem
given	read
laid	some
lower	tired
money	

Circle the 12 misspelled words.
Write them correctly on the lines.

Jack had a prblum yesterday. He wanted to red a good book, so he went to a nyce bookstore. Jack picke out a book and handed his muney to the clerk.

Jack said to the clerk, "This is not the write chanje."

The clerk counted the monny agin. Jack was rite. The clerk gave him some more mony, and Jack went home to reed his book.

______________	______________	______________
______________	______________	______________
______________	______________	______________
______________	______________	______________

Word Meaning

Fill in the missing words.

again	change	disagree	does	given
laid	lower	money	nice	of
other	problem	read	some	tired

1. ____________ Arthur have enough ____________ to buy a ticket?
2. Did the ____________ lady help you solve your ____________?
3. I ____________ with what I just ____________ in the newspaper.
4. My hen ____________ some ____________ her eggs in the weeds behind the chicken coop.
5. Harry was ____________ five dollars for cutting Mrs. Murphy's lawn.
6. Would you like to have ____________ of my chocolate bar?

My Spelling Dictation

Write the sentences. Circle the spelling words.

1. ____

2. ____

Word Study

Underline the words that have the schwa sound.
Circle the letters that make the sound.

about lesson

1. disagree	6. tired	11. problem
2. again	7. given	12. used
3. lower	8. nice	13. silent
4. laid	9. read	14. those
5. change	10. raise	15. tiny

Fill in the blank with a rhyming spelling word.

other	money	read	laid
change	nice	tired	some

1. arrange ______________
2. fired ______________
3. honey ______________
4. paid ______________
5. bread ______________
6. twice ______________
7. brother ______________
8. drum ______________

Building Spelling Skills WEEK 20

Spelling List

This Week's Focus:

- Spell words with the variant sounds of **g** and **c**

STEP 1 **Read and Spell**

STEP 2 **Copy and Spell**

STEP 3 **Cover and Spell**

fold

1. city
2. cereal
3. face
4. could
5. guess
6. huge
7. age
8. danger
9. goose
10. gone
11. coast
12. clean
13. guard
14. giant
15. carton
16. ______ bonus word
17. ______ bonus word

Visual Memory

Find the words hiding in this puzzle.

c	e	r	e	a	l	a	g	e	d	o
g	i	g	u	a	r	d	o	m	a	c
u	o	t	c	a	r	t	o	n	n	o
e	x	n	y	c	e	r	s	h	g	u
s	s	e	e	f	a	c	e	u	e	l
s	a	n	g	i	a	n	t	g	r	d
c	o	a	s	t	q	c	l	e	a	n

age	face
carton	giant
cereal	gone
city	goose
clean	guard
coast	guess
could	huge
danger	

Circle the misspelled words.
Write them correctly on the lines.

1. age	6. koast	11. gawn
2. cartun	7. could	12. goose
3. sereal	8. danjer	13. gard
4. citee	9. fase	14. guess
5. clean	10. giant	15. huje

Word Meaning

Fill in the missing words.

coast	city	age	guess
danger	clean	guard	giant

1. The movie star had a ______________ to protect her.
2. Have you ever been to New York ______________?
3. The warning sign read "______________! Falling rocks."
4. The magician could ______________ a person's ______________.
5. Did you help ______________ up the beach on Saturday?
6. Why does she always buy ______________-sized packages of everything?
7. I can see sailboats off the ______________.

My Spelling Dictation

Write the sentences. Circle the spelling words.

1. ____

____

____

2. ____

____

____

Word Study

The letters **c** and **g** make a hard and a soft sound.

Read each word and listen to the sound of the bolded letter.
Write it in the correct box.

a**g**e	**g**iant	**c**lean	**c**oast	fa**c**e
carton	**g**one	**g**uess	**c**ould	**g**oose
cereal	**c**ity	hu**g**e	dan**g**er	**g**uard

c		g	
hard /**k**/	soft /**s**/	hard /**g**/	soft /**j**/

Fill in the blanks with spelling words that mean the opposite.

1. country ______________
2. tiny ______________
3. safety ______________
4. dirty ______________

Fill in the missing spelling words and their opposites.

1. When faced with ______________, he ran for ______________.
2. The ______________ goat hid from the ______________ wolf.
3. He was ______________ in class this morning, but is ______________ now.

Building Spelling Skills WEEK 21

Spelling List

This Week's Focus:
- Spell r-controlled words with **or**, **er**, **ir**, **ur**, and **ear**

STEP 1 Read and Spell	STEP 2 Copy and Spell	STEP 3 Cover and Spell
1. word		
2. work		
3. world		
4. were		
5. first		
6. girl		
7. turned		
8. learn		
9. bird		
10. fire		
11. here		
12. nurse		
13. jury		
14. stirred		
15. wear		
16. ______ bonus word		
17. ______ bonus word		

fold

Visual Memory

Unscramble the words. Write them on the lines.

word	were	turned	fire	jury
work	first	learn	here	stirred
world	girl	bird	nurse	wear

1. rowk ____________
2. drow ____________
3. gril ____________
4. laern ____________
5. fier ____________
6. weer ____________
7. nuser ____________
8. brid ____________
9. rowld ____________
10. yurj ____________
11. frist ____________
12. raew ____________
13. ternud ____________
14. sterrid ____________
15. reeh ____________

Circle the 9 misspelled words.
Write them correctly on the lines.

Raul was on his way to wurk when he tirned a corner and saw a house on frie. Ferst, he called 911. Then, he looked around the house.

Raul herd a gril calling for help. He helped her crawl out a window.

At the hospital, a nurse took good care of the gerl. The child said, "I want to lurn how to be a nurs when I grow up."

____________ ____________ ____________

____________ ____________ ____________

____________ ____________ ____________

Word Meaning

Answer the questions.

word	work	world	were	first
girl	turned	learn	bird	fire
here	nurse	jury	stirred	wear

1. Who helps sick and injured people? ______________
2. Which spelling word means...?
   - the earth ______________
   - flames ______________
   - mixed it up ______________
3. What do you call letters put together to represent something? ______________
4. Who decides if a person is innocent or guilty of a crime? ______________
5. Which spelling word is the opposite of ...?
   - last ______________ boy ______________
   - play ______________ there ______________

My Spelling Dictation

Write the sentences. Circle the spelling words.

1. ____

____

____

2. ____

____

____

Word Study

Circle the letters that make the /**er**/ sound in these words.

1. first	3. turned	5. word	7. faster
2. learn	4. girl	6. were	8. work

Fill in the missing letters to make spelling words. Write **er**, **ir**, **ur**, **ear**, or **or**.

1. n______se	3. w______e	5. l______n	7. w______d
2. b______d	4. w______ld	6. quick______	8. st______red

Write the spelling word that rhymes with each of these words.

word	work	world	were	first
girl	learn	fire	wear	nurse

1. care ________	4. burst ________	7. bird ________
2. fur ________	5. curl ________	8. liar ________
3. clerk ________	6. fern ________	9. purse ________

Fill in the missing spelling words.

1. What are you going to ____________ to the party?
2. Where ____________ the boys going in such a hurry?
3. My dad has to ____________ in the garden this Saturday.
4. Her mother is a ____________ in Dr. Chan's office.

Building WEEK 22 Spelling Skills

Spelling List

This Week's Focus:

- Spell r-controlled words with **ar**, **are**, **or**, and **ore**

STEP 1 Read and Spell	STEP 2 Copy and Spell	STEP 3 Cover and Spell
1. aren't		
2. partner		
3. hard		
4. chart		
5. farm		
6. start		
7. large		
8. more		
9. before		
10. horse		
11. north		
12. morning		
13. care		
14. stare		
15. warning		
16. ______ bonus word		
17. ______ bonus word		

fold

Visual Memory

Match the parts to make a spelling word.
Write the complete word on the line.

1. far	th	1. farm
2. lar	n't	2.
3. nor	m	3.
4. are	re	4.
5. sta	ge	5.
6. warn	fore	6.
7. be	ner	7.
8. part	ing	8.

Circle the misspelled words.
Write them correctly on the lines.

1. arent	6. narth	11. hourse
2. care	7. stayr	12. partnur
3. mor	8. morning	13. hard
4. charte	9. befor	14. warning
5. farm	10. start	15. larje

Word Meaning

Fill in the missing words.

1. His ______________ (partner, start) rode off ______________ (horse, before) daybreak.

2. Is it hard work to run a ______________ (care, large) ______________ (more, farm)?

3. We must ______________ (start, warning) on our trip early in the ______________ (before, morning).

4. Read the ______________ (morning, warning) on the ______________ (start, chart) before you dive in.

5. It isn't polite to ______________ (care, stare) at people.

6. The explorer had a ______________ (north, hard) trip going by dog sled.

My Spelling Dictation

Write the sentences. Circle the spelling words.

1. ____

____

____

2. ____

____

____

Word Study

Fill in the missing letters to make a spelling word.
Write **ar**, **or**, **are**, or **ore**.

1. p__ar__tner
2. n______th
3. m______ning
4. c______
5. h______d
6. ______en't
7. bef______
8. w______ning
9. st______
10. l______ge
11. m______e
12. ch______t
13. st______t
14. h______se
15. f______m

Write the opposite of each word from your spelling list.

1. easy ____________
2. tiny ____________
3. less ____________
4. after ____________
5. south ____________
6. evening ____________
7. finish ____________

Fill in the missing spelling words and their opposites.

1. The __________ giant and the __________ elf were friends.
2. I take a walk in the __________ and again in the __________.
3. Migrating birds fly __________ in the fall and __________ in the spring.
4. I do my homework __________ dinner, and then I play __________ dinner.

Building Spelling Skills WEEK 23

Spelling List

This Week's Focus:

- Spell words with the vowel sounds in **to**, **top**, **wall**, and **up**
- Recognize homophones **threw** and **through**
- Spell words with suffixes **-less** and **-ful**

STEP 1 Read and Spell	STEP 2 Copy and Spell	STEP 3 Cover and Spell
1. threw	______	______
2. through	______	______
3. thoughtless	______	______
4. caught	______	______
5. fault	______	______
6. taught	______	______
7. because	______	______
8. one	______	______
9. once	______	______
10. water	______	______
11. watch	______	______
12. wanted	______	______
13. wonder	______	______
14. wonderful	______	______
15. walk	______	______
16. ______ bonus word	______	______
17. ______ bonus word	______	______

fold

Visual Memory

Find the words hiding in this puzzle.

w	a	n	t	e	d	e	d	b	e	c
t	h	o	u	g	h	t	l	e	s	s
h	r	t	a	u	g	h	t	c	w	o
r	e	w	a	t	e	r	o	a	o	n
e	w	a	a	n	d	o	o	u	n	c
w	f	a	u	l	t	u	n	s	d	e
w	a	t	c	h	k	g	w	e	e	t
o	n	c	a	u	g	h	t	x	r	e
n	w	o	n	d	e	r	f	u	l	d

because	through
caught	walk
fault	wanted
once	watch
one	water
taught	wonder
thoughtless	wonderful
threw	

Circle the misspelled words.
Write them correctly on the lines.

1. wundir
2. caught
3. walk
4. wunce
5. becuz
6. tawght
7. thoughtless
8. watur
9. through
10. fawlt
11. wanted
12. throo
13. wach
14. onederful
15. one

Word Meaning

Answer the questions.

threw	walk	one	through	wonderful
once	water	wonder	watch	thoughtless
caught	wanted	because	fault	taught

1. Which spelling words rhyme with ...?

   bought ________________ ________________

   new ________________ ________________

2. What does **watch** mean in this sentence? Circle your answer.

   You must watch your step when you climb a ladder.

   a. be careful b. something that tells time c. standing guard

3. Which word means "only one time"? ________________

4. What is the past tense of ...?

   catch ________________ teach ________________

   throw ________________ want ________________

My Spelling Dictation

Write the sentences. Circle the spelling words.

1. ____

   ____

   ____

2. ____

   ____

   ____

Word Study

Read the words. Listen for the vowel sounds.
Write each word in the correct box.

wanted	water	through	walk
threw	because	watch	taught
thought	caught	fault	

sound of **a** in **wall**	sound of **oo** in **too**

Add the correct suffix to the words.

-less means "without"

-ful means "filled with"

1. Morris had a ____________ surprise.
(wonder)

2. It was ____________ of you to be late for the party.
(thought)

3. The ____________ man helped fix the flat tire.
(thought)

4. I always feel ____________ on my birthday.
(joy)

5. A newborn kitten is ____________.
(help)

6. Will you be ____________ and clean up that mess?
(help)

Building Spelling Skills WEEK 24

Spelling List

This Week's Focus:

- Spell words that end with **or**, **ar**, and **er**
- Spell words with the final long **e** sound spelled **y**

STEP 1 Read and Spell	STEP 2 Copy and Spell	STEP 3 Cover and Spell
1. color		
2. odor		
3. farmer		
4. calendar		
5. dollar		
6. party		
7. liar		
8. after		
9. number		
10. better		
11. doctor		
12. weather		
13. every		
14. forty		
15. sugar		
16. ______ bonus word		
17. ______ bonus word		

fold

Visual Memory

Match the parts. Write the words on the lines.

1. co	y	1. color
2. calen	ber	2. ______
3. part	lor	3. ______
4. ev	dar	4. ______
5. num	ery	5. ______
6. o	gar	6. ______
7. doc	dor	7. ______
8. for	tor	8. ______
9. su	ty	9. ______
10. weath	ter	10. ______
11. bet	er	11. ______

Circle the misspelled words. Write them correctly on the lines.

1. The calender cost one doller.

   ______ ______

2. Dad had a big partie when he turned fourty.

   ______ ______

3. You had bettir see the doctur about that bad cold.

   ______ ______

4. What nummer comes after nine?

   ______

5. Evry flower in the garden has a sweet oder.

   ______ ______

Word Meaning

Answer these questions.

color	odor	farmer	dollar	calendar
party	liar	after	number	better
doctor	weather	every	sugar	forty

1. Which letters make the /**er**/ sound in these words?

   liar ______________ after ______________ odor ______________

2. What do you call someone who helps sick people? ______________

3. What do you call someone who is not truthful? ______________

4. Which spelling word has the /**sh**/ sound in **she**? ______________

5. Which spelling word means "all"? ______________

6. What is the opposite of...?

   before ______________ worse ______________

My Spelling Dictation

Write the sentences. Circle the spelling words.

1. ____

   ____

   ____

2. ____

   ____

   ____

Word Study

Underline all the words that have the /**er**/ sound in **her**.
Circle the letters that make the /**er**/ sound.

color	every	better
odor	calendar	sugar
party	watch	dollar
march	number	liar
weather	after	farmer

Divide the words into syllables.

1. color col or
2. calendar ______
3. better ______
4. dollar ______
5. farmer ______
6. number ______
7. party ______
8. liar ______
9. weather ______
10. odor ______
11. after ______
12. sugar ______

Building Spelling Skills WEEK 25

Spelling List

This Week's Focus:

- Spell words with the /**f**/ sound spelled **ph**, **gh**, and **f**
- Spell words with the base word **happy**
- Spell words with the suffixes **-ly** and **-ness**

STEP 1 Read and Spell	STEP 2 Copy and Spell	STEP 3 Cover and Spell
1. phone		
2. photograph		
3. orphan		
4. alphabet		
5. graph		
6. nephew		
7. enough		
8. father		
9. half		
10. Friday		
11. cough		
12. unhappy		
13. happier		
14. happily		
15. happiness		
16. ______ bonus word		
17. ______ bonus word		

fold

Visual Memory

Match the parts to make a spelling word.
Write the complete word on the line.

1. Fri	phan		1. ________
2. fa	ew		2. ________
3. or	day		3. ________
4. neph	nough		4. ________
5. e	ther		5. ________
6. pho	hap	py	6. ________
7. al	to	bet	7. ________
8. un	pha	graph	8. ________

Circle the misspelled words.
Write them correctly on the lines.

1. fone	5. fotograph	9. orfan
2. haf	6. fadder	10. happiness
3. alfabet	7. nefew	11. enuf
4. cough	8. graph	12. Fritay

________ ________ ________

________ ________ ________

________ ________ ________

Word Meaning

Answer the questions.

phone	orphan	nephew	happiness	cough
alphabet	graph	enough	Friday	photograph
father	half	unhappy	happier	happily

1. What do you call a picture taken with a camera? __________
2. What is the word for a child with no parents? __________
3. What is a name for all the letters from **a** to **z**? __________
4. Which spelling word means "all that is needed"? __________
5. What do you do when you have a bad cold? __________
6. Which spelling words are names for family members?

__________ __________

My Spelling Dictation

Write the sentences. Circle the spelling words.

1. __________

2. __________

Word Study

Sometimes the digraph **ph** and **gh** stand for the /**f**/ sound.
Fill in the missing letters. Write **f**, **ph**, or **gh**.

1. ph one
2. enou____
3. or____an
4. ____ather
5. ____riday
6. ne____ew
7. hal____
8. gra____
9. al____abet
10. ____otogra____

Fill in the missing letters to complete the spelling word.

1. Grandmother has an old ph____________ of her mother.
2. The first-grade teacher wrote the ______ph________ on the chalkboard.
3. I ate ________f of the chicken on F__________.

A suffix is something you add to the end of words to change the meaning.
Change these words by adding a suffix.

ly means "in this way" | **ness** means "the state of being"

1. She climbed ______________ (slow) and ______________ (careful) up the ladder.
2. The explorers were surrounded by ______________ (dark) inside the cave.
3. Red Riding Hood skipped along ______________ (happy) to Grandma's house.
4. His ______________ (kind) filled my heart with ______________ (happy).

Building Spelling Skills WEEK 26

Spelling List

This Week's Focus:

- Spell words with silent letters
- Spell words with the prefixes **un-** and **re-**

STEP 1 Read and Spell	STEP 2 Copy and Spell	STEP 3 Cover and Spell
1. ghost		
2. neighbor		
3. high		
4. knew		
5. knot		
6. unknown		
7. rewrap		
8. wrong		
9. written		
10. wrapper		
11. unwrap		
12. climb		
13. limb		
14. gnaw		
15. gnat		
16. ______ bonus word		
17. ______ bonus word		

fold

Visual Memory

Find the words hiding in this puzzle.

g	h	o	s	t	k	n	e	w	z
n	e	i	g	h	b	o	r	r	w
k	x	g	g	i	r	l	e	i	r
n	w	n	n	h	k	i	w	t	a
o	r	o	a	a	g	m	r	t	p
t	o	t	t	s	w	b	a	e	p
u	n	k	n	o	w	n	p	n	e
o	g	u	m	c	l	i	m	b	r
i	n	u	n	w	r	a	p	g	o

climb	neighbor
ghost	rewrap
gnat	unknown
gnaw	unwrap
high	wrapper
knew	written
knot	wrong
limb	

Circle the misspelled words.
Write them correctly on the lines.

1. gost
2. naybor
3. hi
4. gnat
5. knot
6. knoo
7. unknone
8. rewrap
9. rong
10. written
11. onwrap
12. clim
13. limb
14. naw

______ ______ ______

______ ______ ______

______ ______ ______

15. The ribbon was tied in a not. ______
16. Little nats flew around the fruit tree. ______
17. A lim broke off the tree during the storm. ______

Word Meaning

Complete the crossword puzzle.

Across

1. not known
4. to move up a ladder
6. to take off the covering
8. the spirit of someone dead seen by a person
9. a fastening made by tying string together

Down

2. a person who lives next door
3. the opposite of **right**
5. words were put on paper
7. a small insect
8. to chew on

ghost	high	gnaw	limb	knot
written	knew	unknown	unwrap	wrong
rewrap	climb	gnat	neighbor	

My Spelling Dictation

Write the sentences. Circle the spelling words.

1. ______________________________

2. ______________________________

Word Study

Read each word.
Mark an **X** over the silent letters.

wrap knot

ghost	limb	knot	unwrap
high	knew	rewrap	climb
gnaw	write	wrong	gnat

Write the correct prefix in front of each word.

un means "not"
unhappy means "not happy"

re means "again"
reread means "read again"

1. My cat tore the paper on the gift, so Mother had to ______________ it.
(wrap)

2. The name of the artist was ______________.
(known)

3. People were ______________ of what to do after the earthquake.
(sure)

4. My homework paper was messy, so I had to ______________ it.
(write)

5. ______________ the present to see what is inside.
(Wrap)

6. Uncle Ted must ______________ the fence every five years.
(paint)

Building Spelling Skills WEEK 27

Spelling List

This Week's Focus:

- Spell words with the suffixes **-ful**, **-ly**, **-less**, **-er**, and **-est**

STEP 1 Read and Spell | **STEP 2 Copy and Spell** | **STEP 3 Cover and Spell**

(fold)

1. useful
2. quietly
3. slowly
4. careful
5. careless
6. quickly
7. useless
8. worthless
9. fearful
10. fearless
11. joyful
12. smarter
13. fastest
14. funniest
15. happiest
16. ____________ bonus word
17. ____________ bonus word

Visual Memory

Write the missing suffix to make a spelling word.

ful ly less er

1. useful______
2. use______
3. quiet______
4. worth______
5. smart______
6. slow______
7. joy______
8. fast______
9. care______
10. care______
11. fear______
12. fear______

Circle the misspelled words.
Write them correctly on the lines.

1. Mother walked slooly and kwietly past the sleeping baby.

______ ______

2. Carla was joyfull when she won the ribbon for fastist runner in school.

______ ______

3. It is useles to do the job if you are kareless.

______ ______

4. Pete is the happyest person I know.

______

5. A feerless shepherd quikly chased away the hungry wolf.

______ ______

Word Meaning

Answer the questions.

useful	quietly	slowly	careful	quickly
careless	useless	fearful	joyful	worthless
smarter	fastest	fearless	funniest	happiest

1. What do these words do? **smarter** **fastest**
   a. name something b. compare something c. describe something
2. What do these words do? **thoughtless** **useful**
   a. name something b. compare something c. describe something
3. Which spelling word is the opposite of ...?

   quickly ____________ useful ____________

   careless ____________ saddest ____________
4. Which word means "afraid"? ____________

My Spelling Dictation

Write the sentences. Circle the spelling words.

1. ______________________________

____

____

2. ______________________________

____

____

Word Study

Add the suffix **est** to these words.
Mark what you did to change the word.

		no change	double final consonant	change **y** to **i**
1. fast	fastest	✔		
2. happy	________			
3. quick	________			
4. funny	________			
5. sad	________			
6. big	________			
7. smart	________			
8. silly	________			
9. small	________			

Add suffixes to the words to complete the sentences. Write **ful** or **less**.

1. Be care________ as you work so you don't make a care________ mistake.
2. The fear________ firefighter rescued the fear________ boy from the tree.
3. One sock is use________, but two socks are use________.

Building Spelling Skills WEEK 28

Spelling List

This Week's Focus:

- Spell words with the long **a**, long **e**, and short **e** sounds
- Spell words in the **-other**, **-ead**, **-eat**, and **-ear** word families
- Recognize the /**ur**/ sound in **heard** and **early**

STEP 1 Read and Spell	STEP 2 Copy and Spell	STEP 3 Cover and Spell
1. brother	______	______
2. mother	______	______
3. another	______	______
4. field	______	______
5. friend	______	______
6. heard	______	______
7. early	______	______
8. friendly	______	______
9. head	______	______
10. near	______	______
11. year	______	______
12. shield	______	______
13. eat	______	______
14. measure	______	______
15. break	______	______
16. ______ (bonus word)	______	______
17. ______ (bonus word)	______	______

fold

Visual Memory

Find the words hiding in this puzzle.

m	e	a	s	u	r	e	e	a	a
o	n	e	h	e	a	r	d	n	n
t	r	y	i	e	l	f	s	o	b
h	x	n	e	n	d	i	e	t	r
e	e	e	l	a	h	e	a	h	e
r	a	a	d	o	r	l	r	e	a
n	t	r	d	e	a	d	l	r	k
f	r	i	e	n	d	l	y	o	r
a	n	o	b	r	o	t	h	e	r

another	head
break	heard
brother	measure
early	mother
eat	near
field	shield
friendly	year

Circle the misspelled words. Write them correctly on the lines.

1. My muther and bruther have the same birthday.

_______________ _______________

2. Trina hurd from an old frend today.

_______________ _______________

3. We herd a noise in the empty feeld next door.

_______________ _______________

4. Erly next yeer they are moving to Texas.

_______________ _______________

5. May I eta unother slice of pie?

_______________ _______________

Word Meaning

Complete the crossword puzzle.

Across

1. close by
3. the opposite of **sister**
7. a female parent
10. a piece of armor
12. listened to
13. a person who knows and likes another person

Down

2. the opposite of **late**
4. to chew and swallow food
5. to find the size of something
6. the top part of your body
8. to smash
9. an open area with few trees
11. January 1 to December 31

break	brother	friend	field	near
head	heard	measure	year	
shield	mother	eat	early	

My Spelling Dictation

Write the sentences. Circle the spelling words.

1. ______________________________

____

____

2. ______________________________

____

____

Word Study

Read the words. Listen for the vowel sounds.
Write the words in the correct boxes.

eat	friend	break	measure
head	field	shield	

long **e**	long **a**	short **e**

Change the beginning sounds to create new words.

___m___other	______ead	______eat	______ear
______other	______ead	______eat	______ear
______other	______ead	______eat	______ear
______other	______ead	______eat	______ear

Building Spelling Skills WEEK 29

Spelling List

This Week's Focus:

- Recognize homophones
- Review words with long vowel sounds

STEP 1 Read and Spell	STEP 2 Copy and Spell	STEP 3 Cover and Spell
1. they're		
2. there		
3. their		
4. soup		
5. night		
6. knight		
7. right		
8. write		
9. weight		
10. wait		
11. piece		
12. peace		
13. hour		
14. our		
15. wrote		
16. ______ bonus word		
17. ______ bonus word		

fold

Visual Memory

Match the scrambled word to the correct spelling.

1. ecape	their	7. twai	right
2. ousp	soup	8. peice	wait
3. threi	there	9. rou	piece
4. heret	peace	10. hrou	wrote
5. ightn	write	11. ritgh	hour
6. ritwe	night	12. rwote	our

Circle the misspelled words. Write them correctly on the lines.

1. Their going to get they're books.

   ________________ ________________

2. The brave night saved a princess last nite.

   ________________ ________________

3. Mom said to weight here for an howr.

   ________________ ________________

4. Hour friends came to dinner last nitgh.

   ________________ ________________

5. May I have a peace of there pizza?

   ________________ ________________

6. Can you right a recipe for that soop?

   ________________ ________________

Word Meaning

Fill in the missing words.

1. Can you put ____________ (their, there) coats in the closet over ____________ (they're, there)?

2. The ____________ (knight, night)'s fight lasted all ____________ (knight, night) long.

3. Try to ____________ (right, write) the spelling word ____________ (right, write) this time.

4. We spent an ____________ (our, hour) with ____________ (our, hour) grandfather.

5. What is the ____________ (wait, weight) of that huge hog?

6. That ____________ (peace, piece) of paper is a ____________ (peace, piece) treaty.

My Spelling Dictation

Write the sentences. Circle the spelling words.

1. ____

____

____

2. ____

____

____

Word Study

Read the words. Listen for the vowel sounds.
Write the words in the correct boxes.
Circle the letters that spell the sounds.

wait	peace	night	right	piece	stare
write	weight	beach	stair	sight	plane
flee	knight	plain	beech	flea	site

long **a**	long **i**	long **e**
wait		

Write the opposite of each word from the spelling list.

1. erase ____________
2. day ____________
3. here ____________
4. left ____________
5. war ____________
6. whole ____________

Fill in the missing words.

1. If you ____________ the word wrong, make it ____________.
2. The generals signed the ____________ treaty late one ____________.

Building Spelling Skills WEEK 30

Spelling List

This Week's Focus:

- Review long and short vowel sounds
- Review how to divide words into syllables

STEP 1 Read and Spell	STEP 2 Copy and Spell	STEP 3 Cover and Spell
1. air		
2. against		
3. all right		
4. until		
5. presents		
6. beautiful		
7. favorite		
8. clothes		
9. people		
10. vacation		
11. remember		
12. already		
13. hospital		
14. minute		
15. straight		
16. ______ bonus word		
17. ______ bonus word		

fold

Visual Memory

Match the parts to make spelling words.
Write the complete words on the lines.

1. a	ents		1. ________
2. un	ute		2. ________
3. pres	gainst		3. ________
4. peo	til		4. ________
5. min	ple		5. ________
6. beau	ca	ber	6. ________
7. va	read	ful	7. ________
8. re	ti	tal	8. ________
9. al	pi	y	9. ________
10. hos	mem	tion	10. ________

Circle the misspelled words.
Write them correctly on the lines.

1. air	6. bootiful	11. already
2. alright	7. favrute	12. remimber
3. strate	8. clothes	13. hospital
4. against	9. peeple	14. minite
5. presunts	10. vacashun	15. until

________ ________ ________

________ ________ ________

________ ________ ________

Word Meaning

Complete the crossword puzzle.

Down

1. a place for the care of the sick or injured
2. not crooked
3. very pretty
5. men, women, and children
6. the one you like best

Across

4. gifts
7. a time of rest from school or work
8. what people wear
9. happened before this time
10. don't forget

already	clothes	people	remember	hospital
beautiful	favorite	presents	straight	vacation

My Spelling Dictation

Write the sentences. Circle the spelling words.

1. ______________________________

____

____

2. ______________________________

____

____

Word Study

Circle the letters in the words that make the given sound.

short u	until		
short i	minute	until	
long i	all right		
long o	clothes		
long e	already	remember	
long a	favorite	straight	vacation

Divide the words into syllables.

1. against a gainst
2. presents ______
3. beautiful ______
4. favorite ______
5. people ______
6. vacation ______
7. minute ______
8. hospital ______
9. already ______
10. remember ______

Note: Use this form to track students' spelling progress.

Spelling Record Sheet

Building Spelling Skills

Students' Names																	
1																	
2																	
3																	
4																	
5																	
6																	
7																	
8																	
9																	
10																	
11																	
12																	
13																	
14																	
15																	
16																	
17																	
18																	
19																	
20																	
21																	
22																	
23																	
24																	
25																	
26																	
27																	
28																	
29																	
30																	

Note: Reproduce this form twice for each student to track his or her progress.

My Spelling Record

Building Spelling Skills

Spelling List	Date	Number Correct	Words Missed

Note: Reproduce this form for the end-of-the-week test.

Spelling Test

Listen to the words.
Write each word on a line.

1. ______________________
2. ______________________
3. ______________________
4. ______________________
5. ______________________
6. ______________________
7. ______________________
8. ______________________
9. ______________________
10. ______________________
11. ______________________
12. ______________________
13. ______________________
14. ______________________
15. ______________________
16. ______________________
17. ______________________

Listen to the sentences.
Write them on the lines.

1. ____

____

____

2. ____

____

____

Building **Spelling** Skills

Spelling List

Note: Reproduce this form to make your own spelling list.

Step 1 Read and Spell	Step 2 Copy and Spell	Step 3 Cover and Spell
1.		
2.		
3.		
4.		
5.		
6.		
7.		
8.		
9.		
10.		
11.		
12.		
13.		
14.		
15.		
16.		
17.		

fold

Note: Reproduce this form to make your own word search or crossword puzzles.

Word Box

Note: Reproduce this letter to send home with spelling lists.

Building Spelling Skills

Dear Parents,

Attached is your child's spelling list for this week. Encourage him or her to practice the words in one or more of these ways:

1. Read and spell each word. Cover it up and write it. Uncover the word and check to see if it is correct.
2. Find the words on the spelling list in printed materials such as books and magazines.
3. Read a word aloud and ask your child to spell it (either aloud or written on paper).

Thank you for your support of our spelling program.

Sincerely,

Building Spelling Skills

Dear Parents,

Attached is your child's spelling list for this week. Encourage him or her to practice the words in one or more of these ways:

1. Read and spell each word. Cover it up and write it. Uncover the word and check to see if it is correct.
2. Find the words on the spelling list in printed materials such as books and magazines.
3. Read a word aloud and ask your child to spell it (either aloud or written on paper).

Thank you for your support of our spelling program.

Sincerely,

Student Spelling Dictionaries

Building Spelling Skills

Self-made spelling dictionaries provide students with a reference for words they frequently use in their writing.

Materials

- copy of "My Own Spelling Dictionary" form (page 147)
- 26 sheets of lined paper—6" x 9" (15 x 23 cm)
- 2 sheets of construction paper or tagboard for cover—6" x 9" (15 x 23 cm)
- crayons or markers
- glue
- stapler
- masking tape

Steps to Follow

1. Color and cut out the cover sheet form. Glue it to the front cover of the dictionary.

2. Staple the lined paper inside the cover. Place masking tape over the staples.

3. Guide students (or ask parent volunteers) to write a letter of the alphabet on each page.

What to Include

1. When students ask for the correct spelling of a special word, have them write it in their dictionary.
2. Include special words being learned as part of science or social studies units.
3. Include words for special holidays.
4. Include the common words students continue to misspell on tests and in daily written work.
5. Add color and number words if these are not on charts posted in the classroom.

Building Spelling Skills

My Own

Spelling Dictionary

Name ______________________________

Building Spelling Skills

My Own

Spelling Dictionary

Name ______________________________

You are a SUPER SPELLER!

Name

Congratulations!!

Master Word List

about
above
added
afraid
after
again
against
age
air
alike
alive
all right
almost
along
alphabet
already
also
always
another
April
aren't
around
ask
away
awful
babies
balloon
basketball
beautiful
because
become
been
before
believe
below
better
between
bird
blew
blue
both
bought
boy
brain
break
brook
brother
brought
buy
calendar
called
came
can't
care
careful
careless
carry
carton
catch
caught
cereal
change
chart
chew
children
chocolate
choice
choose
city
clean
climb
close
clothes
coach
coast
coin
color
coming
cookie
cough
could
country
cousin
cried
cry
cube
cute
danger
dear
destroy
didn't
different
disagree
do
doctor
does
doesn't
doing
dollar
don't
drawing
drink
due
early
earthquake
easy
eat
eight
ended
enjoy
enough
even
every
everybody
everyone
everywhere
eye
face
falling
family
farm
farmer
fastest
father
fault
favorite
fearful
fearless
few
field
finally
find
finish
fire
first
float
follow
food
football
forty
found
Friday
friend
friendly
fuel
full
funniest
future
getting
ghost
giant
girl
give
given
gnat
gnaw
gone
good
goose
graph
great
ground
group
grow
grown
guard
guess
half
happened
happening
happier
happiest
happily
happiness
hard
have
having
head
heard
hello
help
here
high
hold
homework
horse
hospital
hour
house
huge
human
I
I'll
I'm
into
it's
its
joined
joked
joyful
jury
kind
knew
knight
knot
know
ladies
lady
laid
large
learn
leave
left
let's
letter
liar
life
light
limb
live
longer
looked
lower
loyal
mall

many
maybe
mean
measure
menu
middle
might
minute
missed
Mississippi
money
more
morning
most
mother
move
much
music
my
myself
near
neighbor
nephew
new
next
nice
niece
night
north
number
nurse
o'clock
odor
of
off
often
oily
once
one
only
open
orphan
other
our
outside

over
own
oyster
partner
party
pattern
peace
people
phone
photograph
piece
pitch
playing
please
pocket
pointing
poison
presents
pretty
prey
price
problem
push
put
quickly
quietly
raise
reached
read
received
remember
rewrap
right
rocket
room
rough
said
save
school
sea
search
seen
sew
she
shield

shoes
short
should
show
shy
silent
skateboard
slowly
small
smarter
smiled
smiling
so
some
something
song
soup
spelling
stand
stare
start
started
stayed
still
stirred
stood
story
straight
straw
strongest
studied
study
such
sugar
sure
surprise
surprises
swam
swim
swimming
takes
taught
teacher
than
that's

their
there
these
they
they're
think
those
thoughtless
three
threw
throne
through
tiny
tired
to
today
together
told
too
touch
tough
town
toys
tried
true
truth
try
turned
two
under
unhappy
uniform
unit
unknown
until
unwrap
upon
use
used
useful
useless
usually
vacation
very
voice

voyage
wait
walk
wanted
warning
watch
water
waved
way
we
wear
weather
weight
were
we're
where
which
while
white
who
whole
why
willing
with
without
won't
wonder
wonderful
word
work
world
worthless
would
wouldn't
wrapper
write
written
wrong
wrote
year
you
young
your
you're
zipper

Note: Corresponding Student Practice Book pages are indicated in parentheses.

Answer Key

Page 21 *(Page 5)*

1. afraid 2. eight 3. away
4. ask 5. great 6. takes
7. than 8. said 9. always
10. they 11. catch 12. prey

These words should be crossed out:

1. sed
2. eitgh
3. grait
4. drey
5. catsh
6. ufraid
7. wavd
8. thay
9. aks
10. stend
11. paling
12. taks
13. fhan
14. uway

Page 22 *(Page 6)*

1. eight, prey
2. takes, catch
3. always, afraid
4. They, playing
5. waved, said
6. stand, away

Page 23 *(Page 7)*

waved	catch	away	takes	great
ask	eight	stand	said	they
always	afraid	prey	than	playing

1. played playing
2. asked asking
3. preyed preying
4. painted painting

1. waved waving
2. smiled smiling
3. skated skating
4. baked baking

Page 25 *(Page 9)*

1. between or believe 2. leave
3. easy, many, or very
4. many, easy, or very
5. please 6. three 7. help
8. she 9. believe or between
10. very, many, or easy
11. seen 12. next

These words should be circled:

1. Plez Please
2. leaf leave
3. eezy easy
4. ben been
5. betwene between
6. belive believe
7. miny many
8. tree three

Page 26 *(Page 10)*

1. three
2. sea
3. a. easy
   b. left
   c. many
   d. leave
   e. help
4. between
5. please
6. believe

Page 27 *(Page 11)*

three	left	she
please	believe	many
very	been	seen
help	between	leave
easy	sea	next

1. very
2. many
3. please
4. sea, she, or three
5. help
6. she, sea, or three
7. seen or between
8. believe
9. three, she, or sea
10. between or seen

Page 29 *(Page 13)*

1. while
2. buy or try
3. light
4. my
5. life
6. swim
7. which
8. eye
9. drink
10. pitch
11. kind or find
12. why

These words should be circled:

1. bie lite buy light
2. Witch drenk Which drink
3. Trie picth Try pitch
4. aye swem eye swim
5. Eye by I buy

Page 30 *(Page 14)*

1. I, eye
2. Why, buy, drink
3. Which, light
4. while, pitch
5. my, try
6. kind, life

Page 31 *(Page 15)*

life	drink	try
pitch	while	I
my	light	buy
eye	which	find
why	kind	swim

Answers will vary but could include:

ind	ile	ight	ink
find	mile	bright	rink
kind	file	light	wink
rind	while	might	pink
mind	smile	tight	link
blind	tile	sight	think
bind	pile	fight	drink

Page 33 *(Page 17)*

1. pocket 2. almost 3. grow
4. open 5. often 6. coach 7. most
8. also 9. throne
10. hold, told, or both 11. rocket
12. sew

These words should be crossed out:

1. roket
2. whold
3. offen
4. thone
5. amolst
6. bofh
7. koach
8. allso
9. opun
10. groe
11. tole
12. sowe

Page 34 *(Page 18)*

1. throne
2. pocket
3. told, hold
4. so, sew
5. open
6. rocket

Page 35 *(Page 19)*

grow	hold	throne
rocket	so	pocket
told	also	sew
most	often	almost
both	coach	open

One syllable	Two syllables
1. grow	1. rocket
2. told	2. also
3. hold	3. often
4. so	4. pocket
5. sew	5. open
6. both	6. almost
7. coach	
8. throne	
9. most	

Page 37 *(Page 21)*

1. much
2. touch
3. use
4. you
5. unit
6. few
7. fuel
8. under
9. such
10. human
11. music
12. young

These words should be circled:

1. undar under
2. noo new
3. yer your
4. kute cute
5. tuch touch
6. yung young
7. fuo few
8. moosic music

Page 38 *(Page 22)*

Pictures will vary but must reflect sentence meaning.

Page 39 *(Page 23)*

use	such	few
young	music	under
your	you	unit
cute	much	new
fuel	human	touch

1. much, such, or touch
2. young
3. under
4. use
5. few, you, or new
6. cute
7. new or you
8. fuel
9. such, much, or touch
10. your

1. under, thunder
2. few, new
3. cute, flute

Page 41 *(Page 25)*

too	alike	blew	know
blue	two	to	do
above	move	save	have
give	live	alive	

These words should be circled:

1. tow two
2. ulike alike
3. blew blue
4. no know
5. hav have
6. geve give
7. too to
8. Moov Move

Page 42 *(Page 26)*

1. two
2. too
3. to
4. blew
5. blue
6. know
7. no

Page 43 *(Page 27)*

1. give
2. move
3. live
4. know
5. do
6. has
7. save

1. moved
2. know
3. blew
4. saved

alive	different
alike	below
above	dead

Page 45 *(Page 29)*

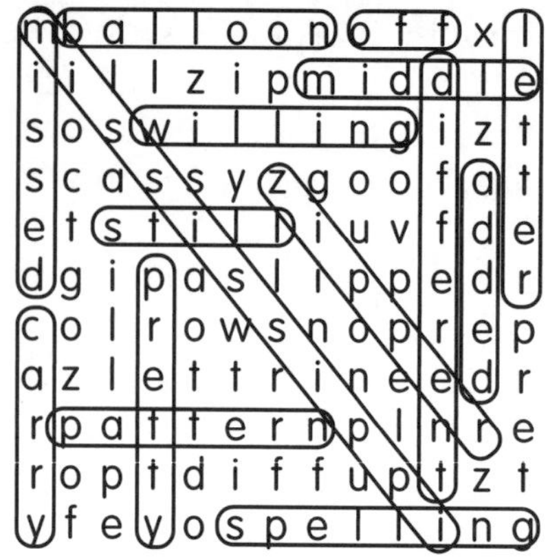

These words should be circled:

1. missed
2. balloon
3. pretty
4. letter
5. different
6. pattern
7. carry
8. zipper

Page 46 *(Page 30)*

1. spelling
2. Mississippi
3. balloon
4. zipper
5. carry
6. letter
7. different or middle
8. pattern

Page 47 *(Page 31)*

1. bal loon
2. spell ing
3. pret ty
4. let ter
5. add ed
6. pat tern
7. zip per
8. will ing
9. mid dle
10. car ry
11. miss ing
12. Mis sis sip pi

1. spelling
2. off
3. still
4. middle
5. pattern
6. missed
7. different
8. Mississippi

Page 49 *(Page 33)*

1. mm
2. m
3. tt
4. t
5. d
6. pp
7. l
8. ll
9. m
10. m
11. k
12. v

1. swimming
2. getting
3. coming
4. having
5. doing
6. happened
7. happening
8. joked
9. smiled
10. came

1. started
2. received
3. smiling

Page 50 *(Page 34)*

1. swam
2. swimming
3. happening
4. happened
5. coming
6. came
7. smiled
8. smiling

Page 51 *(Page 35)*

1. joked
2. swam
3. happened
4. came
5. ended
6. smiled
7. received
8. started

1. swimming—double *m*
2. getting—double *t*
3. receiving—drop *e*
4. coming—drop *e*
5. having—drop *e*
6. doing—no change
7. smiling—drop *e*
8. ending—no change
9. happening—no change
10. starting—no change
11. joking—drop *e*

Page 53 *(Page 37)*

yaw	close
thees	niece
neice	way
hows	these
anme	tried
locse	mean
deirt	show

beuc	price
ripce	float
mitgh	cube
foalt	uniform
niarb	brain
formuni	stayed
edstay	might

1. youniform — uniform
2. Cloze — Close
3. mite — might
4. kube — cube
5. staid — stayed
6. tryed — tried
7. shoo — show
8. flote — float

Page 54 *(Page 38)*

Across
1. mean
4. price
5. uniform
8. close
9. these

Down
2. niece
3. brain
6. float
7. cube
10. stay

Page 55 *(Page 39)*

1. way a
2. these e
3. niece e
4. show o
5. float o
6. brain a
7. mean e
8. close o
9. tried i
10. cube u
11. uniform u
12. stayed a
13. price i

1. stayed—no change
2. tried—*y* to *i*
3. floated—no change
4. showed—no change
5. cried—*y* to *i*
6. hurried—*y* to *i*
7. planted—no change
8. worried—*y* to *i*
9. played—no change
10. scurried—*y* to *i*

Page 57 *(Page 41)*

These words should be circled:

children	with	search
think	push	where
whole	sure	who
		teacher

These words should be circled:

1. Hoo — Who
   hole — whole
2. childrun — children
   poosh — push
3. finnish — finish
   shurt — short
4. fink — think
   serch — search
5. teecher — teacher
   togepher — together

Page 58 *(Page 42)*

1. teacher, children
2. everywhere
3. think
4. finish
5. search
6. whole, short, together

Page 59 *(Page 43)*

1. children
2. search
3. think
4. whole
5. where
6. finish
7. together
8. push
9. teacher
10. with
11. short
12. who

1. 3	6. 1	11. 1
2. 1	7. 1	12. 2
3. 1	8. 3	13. 1
4. 2	9. 1	14. 1
5. 1	10. 2	15. 1

Page 61 *(Page 45)*

e v e r y b o d y e s s
v a n h o m e w o r k o
e r r t o d a y m a a m
r w i t h o u t y b t e
y o u i h e r o s e e t
o u t n o q u d e c b h
n e w t t u u y l o o i
e u p o n t o a f m a n
m a y b e m y s k e r g
o u t o u t s i d e d o
b a s k e t b a l l i n

These words should be circled:

homewerk	homework
misef	myself
owtside	outside
skatbord	skateboard
Everbody	Everybody
baskutball	basketball
Evrywon	Everyone
sumthing	something
erthquak	earthquake
wifout	without

Page 62 *(Page 46)*

1. basketball or skateboard
2. earthquake
3. homework, today
4. Something, into
5. upon
6. become
7. without
8. Everyone or Everybody, myself

Page 63 *(Page 47)*

1. basketball
2. become
3. earthquake
4. everybody
5. everyone
6. homework
7. into
8. myself
9. maybe
10. outside
11. skateboard
12. something
13. today
14. upon
15. without

1. in|to
2. to|day
3. with|out
4. be|come
5. some|thing
6. may|be
7. out|side
8. home|work
9. earth|quake

Yes—Divide compound words into syllables between smaller words.

Page 65 *(Page 49)*

1. awful
2. called
3. mall
4. song
5. small
6. along
7. rough
8. longer
9. straw
10. drawing
11. strongest
12. falling

These words should be circled:

1. ahful		awful
2. smal	starw	small straw
3. drawn	stronust	drawing strongest
4. bawght	moll	bought mall
5. longar	sogn	longer song

Page 66 *(Page 50)*

1. awful
2. straw
3. mall
4. drawing
5. bought, small — longer, strongest
6. b

Page 67 *(Page 51)*

awful	called	tough
mall	song	along
rough	bought	straw
strongest	falling	brought
small	drawing	longer

1. stronger — strongest
2. longer — longest
3. smaller — smallest
4. rougher — roughest
5. tougher — toughest

6. strongest
7. smaller
8. roughest
9. toughest
10. longer

Page 69 *(Page 53)*

1. lady
2. family
3. only
4. surprises
5. ladies
6. study
7. finally
8. story
9. studied
10. surprise

These words should be circled:

1. suprise	surprise
2. shoos	shoes
3. cryed	cried
4. famuly	family
5. ladys	ladies
6. storie	story
7. finelly	finally
8. studyed	studied

Page 70 *(Page 54)*

1. surprise
2. ladies
3. finally
4. study
5. surprises
6. cried

Page 71 *(Page 55)*

y says i	y says e
cry	lady
shy	study
why	only
fly	story
my	family
try	funny

Note: Some children find the idea of dropping silent *e* before adding *es* confusing. You may choose to accept "add *s*" as correct answers for numbers 4 and 7.

1. ladies - *y* to *i*, add *es*
2. toys - add *s*
3. stories - *y* to *i*, add *es*
4. shoes - drop *e*, add *es*
5. families - *y* to *i*, add *es*
6. rockets - add *s*
7. nieces - drop *e*, add *es*

Page 73 *(Page 57)*

f	g	t	r	u	t	h	c	h	f
l	o	o	k	e	d	r	o	c	u
f	o	o	d	o	o	k	o	o	l
t	d	p	t	c	h	e	w	o	l
r	u	u	u	b	r	o	o	k	m
u	e	s	p	t	a	t	h	i	h
e	s	c	h	o	o	l	x	e	e
n	o	s	f	o	o	d	l	m	w

These words should be circled:

1. luked	looked
4. futbal	football
5. cookee	cookie
6. fud	food
8. poot	put
10. schol	school
12. doo	due
13. chu	chew
15. ruum	room

Page 74 *(Page 58)*

Across	Down
1. food	1. full
3. football	2. cookie
7. brook	4. truth
9. chew	5. looked
10. good	6. true
	8. school

Page 75 *(Page 59)*

u in **push**	**o** in **do**
looked	food
good	school
brook	truth
football	room
cookie	true
stood	chew
full	due
put	

1. full
2. good
3. stood
4. put
5. truth
6. true

Page 77 *(Page 61)*

1. yoil	voice
2. cevoi	oily
3. soyter	boy
4. joyen	voyage
5. yob	oyster
6. agevoy	loyal
7. loyla	enjoy
8. ocin	coin
9. ingpoint	joined
10. cocholate	choice
11. edjoin	chocolate
12. oichce	pointing
13. sonpoi	destroy
14. troydes	poison

These words should be circled:

1. choyse	choice
chocklate	chocolate
2. injoy	enjoy
voyege	voyage
3. distroy	destroy
poisen	poison
4. doy	boy
oister	oyster
5. coyn	coin
chose	choose

Page 78 *(Page 62)*

1. oysters, voyage
2. Chocolate, choice
3. boy, destroy
4. pointing, coin
5. voice
6. poison

Page 79 *(Page 63)*

1. boy
2. oily
3. choice
4. oyster
5. voice
6. loyal
7. poison
8. pointing
9. destroy
10. coin
11. enjoy
12. joined

1. points	pointed	pointing
2. joins	joined	joining
3. smiles	smiled	smiling
4. finishes	finished	finishing

1. smiling
2. points
3. finishes
4. joining

Page 81 *(Page 65)*

1. don't
2. didn't
3. I'll
4. that's
5. it's
6. can't
7. let's
8. you're
9. we're
10. doesn't
11. o'clock
12. won't
13. I'm
14. wouldn't

These words should be circled:

1. din't	didn't
2. were	we're
3. duzn't	doesn't
4. Your	You're
5. Tat's	That's
6. Its	It's
7. kan't	can't
8. A'll	I'll

Page 82 *(Page 66)*

Down	Across
1. can't	4. wouldn't
2. I'll	8. won't
3. doesn't	9. that's
5. don't	10. you're
6. o'clock	11. let's
7. it's	
8. we're	

Page 83 *(Page 67)*

1. will not — do not
2. its
3. I'll

contractions	missing letters
1. don't	o
2. we're	a
3. they're	a
4. it's	i
5. wouldn't	o
6. can't	no
7. I'm	a
8. that's	i
9. doesn't	o
10. didn't	o
11. I'll	wi
12. let's	u

Page 85 *(Page 69)*

1. town
2. house
3. group
4. found
5. follow
6. cousin
7. about
8. own
9. below
10. would
11. around
12. grown
13. country
14. should
15. ground

These words should be circled:

kussin	cousin
grup	group
toun	town
fallowed	followed
bello	below
arownd	around
groun	ground
cuzin's	cousin's
howse	house

Page 86 *(Page 70)*

1. town, ground
2. cousin, country
3. group, house
4. should, grown
5. around
6. own

Page 87 *(Page 71)*

o in **go**	**ow** in **cow**
grown	found
below	town
follow	about
own	ground
	house
	around

oo in **too**	**u** in **up**	**u** in **put**
group	country cousin	would should

1. about
2. house
3. cousin
4. group
5. should would
6. follow below
7. around found
8. own grown

Page 89 *(Page 73)*

1. A — pril
2. e — ven
3. ba — bies
4. si — lent
5. o — ver
6. ti — ny
7. men — u
8. fu — ture

1. April
2. even
3. babies
4. silent
5. over
6. tiny
7. menu
8. future

These words should be circled:

1. babys deer babies dear
2. raize tiney raise tiny
3. sylent Heloo silent Hello
4. Aprul whyte April white
5. yousd thoze used those

Page 90 *(Page 74)*

1. menu
2. future
   over
   used
   hello
   silent
3. change the *y* to *i* and add *es*
4. April

Page 91 *(Page 75)*

long **a**	long **o**	long **e**
raised April babies	over those hello	even we tiny babies

long **i**	long **u**
silent white tiny	used future menu

1. A pril
2. ba bies
3. o ver
4. hel lo
5. e ven
6. la dy
7. si lent
8. ti ny
9. men u
10. fu ture

Bonus: va ca tion

Page 93 *(Page 77)*

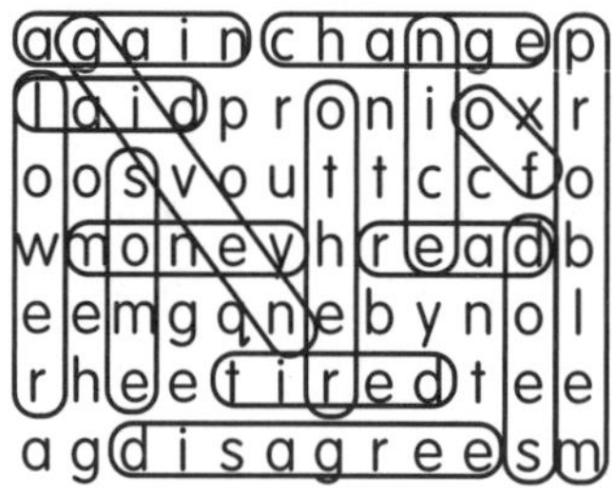

These words should be circled:

prblum	problem
red	read
nyce	nice
picke	picked
muney	money
write	right
chanje	change
monny	money
agin	again
rite	right
mony	money
reed	read

Page 94 *(Page 78)*

1. Does, money
2. nice or other, problem
3. disagree, read
4. laid, of
5. given
6. some

Page 95 *(Page 79)*

1. disagree
2. again
3. lower
4. laid
5. change
6. tired
7. given
8. nice
9. read
10. raise
11. problem
12. used
13. silent
14. those
15. tiny

1. change
2. tired
3. money
4. laid
5. read
6. nice
7. other
8. some

Page 97 *(Page 81)*

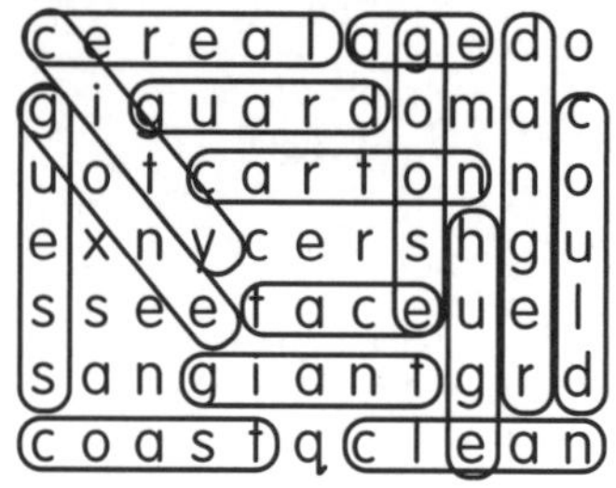

These words should be circled:

2. cartun	carton
3. sereal	cereal
4. citee	city
6. koast	coast
8. danjer	danger
9. fase	face
11. gawn	gone
13. gard	guard
15. huje	huge

Page 98 *(Page 82)*

1. guard
2. City
3. Danger
4. guess, age
5. clean
6. giant
7. coast

Page 99 *(Page 83)*

k	**s**	**g**	**j**
carton	cereal	gone	age
clean	city	goose	danger
coast	face	guard	giant
could		guess	huge

1. city
2. huge or giant
3. danger
4. clean

1. danger, safety
2. tiny, huge or giant
3. present, gone

Page 101 *(Page 85)*

1. work
2. word
3. girl
4. learn
5. fire
6. were
7. nurse
8. bird
9. world
10. jury
11. first
12. wear
13. turned
14. stirred
15. here

These words should be circled:

wurk	work
tirned	turned
frie	fire
Ferst	First
herd	heard
gril	girl
gerl	girl
lurn	learn
nurs	nurse

Page 102 *(Page 86)*

1. nurse
2. world
   fire
   stirred
3. word
4. jury
5. first girl
   work here

Page 103 *(Page 87)*

1. first
2. learn
3. turned
4. girl
5. word
6. were
7. faster
8. work

1. nurse
2. bird
3. were
4. world
5. learn
6. quicker
7. word
8. stirred

1. wear
2. were
3. work
4. first
5. girl
6. learn
7. word
8. fire
9. nurse

1. wear
2. were
3. work
4. nurse

Page 105 *(Page 89)*

1. far	th
2. lar	n't
3. nor	m
4. are	re
5. sta	ge
6. warn	fore
7. be	ner
8. part	ing

1. farm
2. large
3. north
4. aren't
5. stare
6. warning
7. before
8. partner

These words should be circled:

1. arent	aren't
3. mor	more
4. charte	chart
6. narth	north
7. stayr	stare
9. befor	before
11. hourse	horse
12. partnur	partner
15. larje	large

Page 106 *(Page 90)*

1. partner, before
2. large, farm
3. start, morning
4. warning, chart
5. stare
6. hard

Page 107 *(Page 91)*

1. partner
2. north
3. morning
4. care
5. hard
6. aren't
7. before
8. warning
9. stare
10. large
11. more
12. chart
13. start
14. horse
15. farm

1. hard
2. large
3. more
4. before
5. north
6. morning
7. start

1. large, tiny
2. morning, evening
3. south, north
4. before, after

Page 109 *(Page 93)*

w a n t e d e d b e c
t h o u g h t l e s s
h r t a u g h t c w o
r e w a t e r o a o n
e w a a n d o o u n c
w f a u l t u n s d e
w a t c h k g w e e t
o n c a u g h t x r e
n w o n d e r f u l d

These words should be circled:

1. wundir	wonder
4. wunce	once
5. becuz	because
6. tawght	taught
8. watur	water
10. fawlt	fault
12. throo	threw or through
13. wach	watch
14. onederful	wonderful

Page 110 *(Page 94)*

1. caught taught
   threw through
2. a
3. once
4. caught taught
   threw wanted

Page 111 *(Page 95)*

a in **wall**	**oo** in **too**
thought	threw
because	through
caught	
fault	
taught	
wanted	
water	
watch	
walk	

1. wonderful
2. thoughtless
3. thoughtful
4. joyful
5. helpless
6. helpful

Page 113 *(Page 97)*

1. co	y	1. color
2. calen	ber	2. calendar
3. part	lor	3. party
4. ev	dar	4. every
5. num	ery	5. number
6. o	gar	6. odor
7. doc	dor	7. doctor
8. for	tor	8. forty
9. su	ty	9. sugar
10. weath	ter	10. weather
11. bet	er	11. better

These words should be circled:

1. calender	calendar
doller	dollar
2. partie	party
fourty	forty
3. bettir	better
doctur	doctor
4. nummer	number
5. Evry	Every
oder	odor

Page 114 *(Page 98)*

1. liar ar   after er   odor or
2. doctor
3. liar
4. sugar
5. every
6. after   better

Page 115 *(Page 99)*

color	every	better
odor	calendar	sugar
party	watch	dollar
march	number	liar
weather	after	farmer

1. col or	7. par ty
2. cal en dar	8. li ar
3. bet ter	9. weath er
4. dol lar	10. o dor
5. farm er	11. af ter
6. num ber	12. sug ar

Page 117 *(Page 101)*

1. Fri	phan	
2. fa	ew	
3. or	day	
4. neph	nough	
5. e	ther	
6. pho	hap	py
7. al	to	bet
8. un	pha	graph

1. Friday	5. enough
2. father	6. photograph
3. orphan	7. alphabet
4. nephew	8. unhappy

These words should be circled:

1. fone	phone
2. haf	half
3. alfabet	alphabet
5. fotograph	photograph
6. fadder	father
7. nefew	nephew
9. orfan	orphan
11. enuf	enough
12. Fritay	Friday

Page 118 *(Page 102)*

1. photograph
2. orphan
3. alphabet
4. enough
5. cough
6. father, nephew

Page 119 *(Page 103)*

1. phone	6. nephew
2. enough	7. half
3. orphan	8. graph
4. father	9. alphabet
5. Friday	10. photograph

1. photograph
2. alphabet
3. half, Friday

1. slowly, carefully
2. darkness
3. happily
4. kindness, happiness

Page 121 *(Page 105)*

g	h	o	s	t	k	n	e	w	z
n	e	i	g	h	b	o	r	r	w
k	x	g	g	r	i	l	e	i	r
n	w	n	n	h	k	i	w	t	a
o	r	o	a	a	g	m	r	t	p
t	o	t	t	s	w	b	a	e	p
u	n	k	n	o	w	n	p	n	e
o	g	m	u	c	l	i	m	b	r
i	n	u	n	w	r	a	p	g	o

These words should be circled:

1. gost	ghost
2. naybor	neighbor
3. hi	high
6. knoo	knew
7. unknone	unknown
9. rong	wrong
11. onwrap	unwrap
12. clim	climb
14. naw	gnaw
15. not	knot
16. nats	gnats
17. lim	limb

Page 122 *(Page 106)*

Across	**Down**
1. unknown	2. neighbor
4. climb	3. wrong
6. unwrap	5. written
8. ghost	7. gnat
9. knot	8. gnaw

Page 123 *(Page 107)*

ghost	limb	knot	unwrap
high	knew	rewrap	climb
gnaw	write	wrong	gnat

1. rewrap
2. unknown
3. unsure
4. rewrite
5. Unwrap
6. repaint

Page 125 *(Page 109)*

1. useful
2. useless
3. quietly
4. worthless
5. smarter
6. slowly
7. joyful
8. fastest
9. careful
10. careless
11. fearful
12. fearless

These words should be circled:

1. slooly	slowly
kwietly	quietly
2. joyfull	joyful
fastist	fastest
3. useles	useless
kareless	careless
4. happyest	happiest
5. feerless	fearless
quikly	quickly

Page 126 *(Page 110)*

1. b
2. c
3. slowly, careful — useless, happiest
4. fearful

Page 127 *(Page 111)*

1. fastest—no change
2. happiest—*y* to *i*
3. quickest—no change
4. funniest—*y* to *i*
5. saddest—double consonant
6. biggest—double consonant
7. smartest—no change
8. silliest—*y* to *i*
9. smallest—no change

1. careful, careless
2. fearless, fearful
3. useless, useful

Page 129 *(Page 113)*

m e a s u r e e a a
o n e h e a r d n n
t r y i e l f s o b
h x m e n d i e t r
e e e l a h e a h e
r a a d o r l r e a
n t r d e a d l r k
f r i e n d l y o r
a n o b r o t h e r

These words should be circled:

1. muther, bruther	mother, brother
2. hurd, frend	heard, friend
3. herd, feeld	heard, field
4. Erly, yeer	Early, year
5. eta, unother	eat, another

Page 130 *(Page 114)*

Across
1. near
3. brother
7. mother
10. shield
12. heard
13. friend

Down
2. early
4. eat
5. measure
6. head
8. break
9. field
11. year

Page 131 *(Page 115)*

long **e**	long **a**	short **e**
eat	break	head
field		measure
shield		friend

Answers will vary but may include:

other	dead	eat	ear
mother	read	beat	hear
brother	head	seat	near
another	lead	neat	year
smother	thread	wheat	fear

Page 133 *(Page 117)*

1. ecape — peace
2. ousp — soup
3. threi — their
4. heret — there
5. ightn — night
6. ritwe — write
7. twai — wait
8. peice — piece
9. rou — our
10. hrou — hour
11. ritgh — right
12. rwote — wrote

These words should be circled:

1. Their, they're	They're, their
2. night, nite	knight, night
3. weight, howr	wait, hour
4. Hour, nitgh	Our, night
5. peace, there	piece, their
6. right, soop	write, soup

Page 134 *(Page 118)*

1. their, there
2. knight's, night
3. write, right
4. hour, our
5. weight
6. piece, peace

Page 135 *(Page 119)*

long **a**	long **i**	long **e**
weight	night	piece
wait	knight	flee
plain	write	peace
plane	right	beach
stair	sight	flea
stare	site	beech

1. write
2. night
3. there
4. right
5. peace
6. piece

1. write, right
2. peace, night

Page 137 *(Page 121)*

1. a — gainst
2. un — til
3. pres — ents
4. peo — ple
5. min — ute
6. beau — ti — ful
7. va — ca — tion
8. re — mem — ber
9. al — read — y
10. hos — pi — tal

1. against
2. until
3. presents
4. people
5. minute
6. beautiful
7. vacation
8. remember
9. already
10. hospital

These words should be circled:

2. alright	all right
3. strate	straight
5. presunts	presents
6. bootiful	beautiful
7. favrute	favorite
9. peeple	people
10. vacashun	vacation
12. remimber	remember
14. minite	minute

Page 138 *(Page 122)*

Down	Across
1. hospital	4. presents
2. straight	7. vacation
3. beautiful	8. clothes
5. people	9. already
6. favorite	10. remember

Page 139 *(Page 123)*

short **u**—until
short **i**—minute until
long **i**—all right
long **o**—clothes
long **e**—already remember
long **a**—favorite straight vacation

1. a gainst
2. pres ents
3. beau ti ful
4. fa vor ite
5. peo ple
6. va ca tion
7. min ute
8. hos pi tal
9. al read y
10. re mem ber